complete
patio

By Steve Cory and the Editors of Sunset Books • Menlo Park, California

SUNSET BOOKS

VP, GENERAL MANAGER: Richard A. Smeby
VP, EDITORIAL DIRECTOR: Bob Doyle
PRODUCTION DIRECTOR: Lory Day
OPERATIONS DIRECTOR: Rosann Sutherland
MARKETING MANAGER: Linda Barker
ART DIRECTOR: Vasken Guiragossian
SPECIAL SALES: Brad Moses

STAFF FOR THIS BOOK
WRITER: Steve Cory
MANAGING EDITOR: Carrie Dodson Davis
COPY EDITOR: Carol Whiteley
ART DIRECTOR: Alice Rogers
PRINCIPAL PHOTOGRAPHER: Loren Santow
ILLUSTRATORS: Bill Oetinger, Greg Maxson
PRODUCTION SPECIALIST: Linda M. Bouchard
PREPRESS COORDINATOR: Eligio Hernandez
INDEXER: Nanette Cardon
PROOFREADER: David Sweet

We'd like to thank Jerry O'Brien, Ian Worpole,
Anthony Davis, Beverley Bozarth Colgan, and Jim
Kopp for additional illustration used in this book.

COVER: Photograph by Douglas A. Salin,
Copyright © 2002 (www.dougsalin.com).
Furnishings and accessories by Linda Applewhite
& Associates (www.lindaapplewhite.com).

10 9 8 7 6 5 4
First Printing January 2006
Copyright © 2006 Sunset Publishing Corporation,
Menlo Park, CA 94025. Third edition. All rights
reserved, including the right of reproduction in
whole or in part in any form.
Library of Congress Control Number 2005926092
ISBN-13: 978-0-376-01411-5
ISBN-10: 0-376-01411-3
Printed in the United States of America.

For additional copies of *Complete Patio* or any other
Sunset book, call 1-800-526-5111 or visit us at
www.sunset.com.

contents

an outdoor living space

Life is more satisfying when you spend a good chunk of it outdoors, dining with friends, reading, or just relaxing and breathing free. This book will show you lots of ideas for creating an outdoor room that is both appealing and comfortable. The projects sometimes involve hard work, but are also fun because they don't disrupt family life and can be accomplished over the course of several weekends.

a perfect patio

A great patio fits you and your family like a glove. To begin planning such a patio, ponder the way you live as well as the way you'd like to live, then give your imagination free rein. Think about your family's needs and habits. Do you enter-tain frequently outdoors? If so, do you prefer casual or formal enter-taining? Do you cook or dine outside often? How much time do you want to spend gardening and maintaining your yard? Do you have pets that might damage fragile patio plants or furniture?

Next, evaluate your yard's assets and liabilities. Even if you plan to enlist the services of a landscape architect or another professional, you need to have a good understanding of your exist-ing landscape.

Then consider how to bring out the best in your particular site. Can your patio capitalize on a beautiful view? Is your property bounded by woods? Perhaps your design can take advantage of a sunny southern exposure or focus on an especially appealing ele-ment, such as a graceful tree.

Consider, too, how to mini-mize your yard's special problems. Is your lot on a steep slope? How much of the lot is exposed to street traffic and noise? Is humid-ity a problem in your area during summer months? Does your current patio open off the wrong room, get too much sun or shade, or lack sufficient space?

◀ **RUSTIC AND COZY**

Old bricks and distressed furnishings contribute a comfortable feel to this patio. The potting shed and exposed hose make gardening convenient, and are not out of place in this casual setting.

▼ **QUIET AND SERENE**

Ferns and flowers form a graceful frame for this natural stone tile patio. Furnishings in a similar color blend with the floor and fade into the background, letting the foliage take the spotlight.

▶ **STEPPING-STONES**

This yard is home to two seating areas connected by a path made of flagstones set one pace apart. The same type of stone is used for both patios.

◄ **IT ALL FITS**

Everything works together on this patio, where container plants rise up to varying heights, as if to sing in a chorus. The pavers are exposed-aggregate concrete and come in several sizes and shapes.

PROPORTION Your patio should be in scale with your house and garden. As an outdoor room, patios are built on a different scale than indoor rooms. Many patios are traditionally scaled to the size of the living room, but don't be afraid to design something larger. Keep in mind that outdoor furniture usually takes up more room than indoor pieces, and it's a good idea to include containers for plants in your design because they take up a lot

PRINCIPLES OF DESIGN

Chapter 3 of this book gives you the nuts and bolts of patio planning. However, don't get so caught up in practicalities and details that you lose sight of the larger design picture. Landscaping professionals often follow four rules for good landscape design:

UNITY Everything in your patio should look as though it belongs together, and it should blend with your house. The paving materials, the overhead, the screens, the furniture—even the plants—should all complement each other and blend with the house's architectural style. Fortunately, most natural patio materials—stone, brick, lumber, adobe—complement each other,

so it's hard to make a big mistake. However, if you will be using concrete pavers, tile, or paint, take care not to choose materials that clash visually.

VARIETY Variety keeps unity from becoming monotonous. A good design offers an element of surprise: a path that leads from a large main terrace to a more intimate one, an overhead with vines climbing over it, a small fountain that gives dimension to a small space, trees that provide varying degrees of light at different times of day. Feel free to get downright whimsical, folksy, or arty; unusual or even outlandish elements that would look garish indoors often are right at home on a patio.

of space, too. See pages 112–13 for specific ideas on planning a space.

If your lot is so big that you need a large patio to keep everything in scale, create smaller areas within the larger whole. For example, squares of plantings inset in paving will break up a monotonous surface. A trellis, an arbor, or a fence can also be used.

To maintain proportion in a small patio, keep the design simple and uncluttered. Clean lines make the elements seem larger. Stepped planting beds lead the eye up and out of a confined area. Tall vertical screens used to enclose a small area actually make it appear larger, as does solid paving, such as brick, with its small-scale, repetitive pattern.

BALANCE The elements of a patio need to be artfully combined to produce the same visual weight on either side of a center of interest. Balance does not mean symmetry—it means that the space does not feel lopsided. For example, if your patio is shaded on one side by a mature tree, balance the tree's weight with perimeter benches or large planters on the other side. An elaborate barbecue setup on one side of the patio can be nicely balanced with a dining area on the other side.

▼ **RICH WITH DETAILS**
A small patio can pack a large amount of visual delight if you add homemade touches. Here, pebble mosaics were meticulously laid to form a rich tapestry. The gate and arbor, made of many thin pieces, also seem woven rather than built.

◄ **BUILDING AROUND A TREE**
The large oak is a beautifully dominant element in this home's landscape, so the patio was positioned and shaped to take full advantage of the tree's shade and canopy. The seating areas to the left help balance the "weight" of the tree in the overall design.

FOCAL POINTS

A plain patio can become memorable when you add a visually arresting element that both draws attention to itself and ties the whole patio together.

The focal point may be a natural feature. If a venerable tree graces your yard, showcase it by building the patio around it. If your yard has a stunning view of a colorful garden, a lake, or a scenic overlook, build a patio oriented toward that feature, so that people's eyes are drawn to it while walking or sitting.

A focal point may be manmade. If your patio has an unusual curve or other shape or a richly textured paver pattern,

place planters and furniture to show it off to best advantage. Pull your outdoor room together by repeating such a detail in other areas—such as a staircase, countertop, or even the cut rafter end of an overhead.

Garden art is abundantly available these days; spend all the time necessary to find pieces that speak to your soul—or your sense of fun. Small sculptures, "shabby chic" furniture, metal-and-glass lawn ornaments, all can set your patio apart from the ordinary. If possible, select one or two large objects and add smaller pieces that go along with the theme.

The right lighting can make your patio a new place at night

by casting dramatic shadows and highlighting features that may look ordinary during the day. Low-voltage lights are easy to install and easy to move to achieve just the effect you want. See pages 72–75 for lighting techniques and instructions on installing lights.

THE RIGHT MATERIALS

Of course, the paving and building materials you choose go a long way toward defining the look and feel of your patio and any vertical structures. New products are always appearing on the market—for instance, concrete pavers that effectively mimic the look of natural stone. The variety of quarried stone and tile has also never been better: exotic slate from India, Mexico, or China; bluestone from the East Coast; adobe from the Southwest.

▲ *ORIENTED TOWARD THE VIEW*
This patio and deck combination is built to face a stunning bay view. Plexiglas panels make for a see-through railing.

◀ **THE RIGHT MOOD**

The interesting plants assembled around this gravel patio have an artistic ambiance accented by a well-chosen garden sculpture.

▼ **WALL ART**

The brick wall facing this patio has been transformed into a work of art by the addition of an antique-looking wall fountain. The fountain is flanked by wisps of bamboo and accented with upturned lights.

▲ **SIMPLE BUT ELEGANT**

This classic flagstone patio is nestled in a leafy setting with a rustic lounge chair and a whimsical planter to add interest.

▶ **ADOBE SETTING**

A large handmade adobe oven is certainly the center of attention here. Benches are also molded out of adobe. Shining through an overhead of trimmed branches, the midday sun casts striking shadows.

casual style

If you think of your patio as the place to kick off your shoes and let down your hair, you may prefer surfaces that are slightly imperfect and natural materials that mingle with abundant foliage.

Informal styles tend toward curves, asymmetry, and apparent randomness. These patios are often easy to maintain because you're not after a scrubbed-clean look. Adjacent plantings can have an informal, slightly overgrown look. You can create an informal patio using many classic paving materials, especially if you lay them in a casual manner. For instance, you can lay a flagstone patio with ragged edges (that is, with no edging) or install large paving units with wide joints to permit moss or other greenery to grow in them. Large adobe blocks, bluestone slabs, and 2-foot-square concrete pavers, which have grown in popularity in recent years, are particularly suited to this kind of installation. Chunks of used concrete—the older, the better—are also good choices.

An informal look is often achieved by choosing furniture that is slightly worn, or at least worn looking. If you place a good number of potted plants near the furniture, you almost can't miss achieving a pleasantly rustic look.

▲ **COLORFULLY YOURS**
Bold contrasting colors add spice to this rough stone patio. Inexpensive painted furniture and small sculptures splash across the surface; a big bouquet of bright flowers provides a complementary backdrop.

▶ **AN INFORMAL TONE**
Prominent crevice plants poke through a concrete paver patio. The informal feel of the landscape is reinforced by the low stone wall that curves around a rustic bench.

▼ IN HARMONY WITH NATURE

Is it a patio or a series of stepping-stones? Wide joints between the stones are filled with bushy blue star creeper, yielding a walking area that blends in seamlessly with its natural setting.

▲ STEPPING INTO A GARDEN

A simple painted bench is nearly engulfed with potted plants. The foliage is arranged vertically to create a lush wall that provides privacy and a pleasant backdrop for conversation. A sprouting shoe adds a touch of whimsy.

◀ A PRIVATE JUNGLE

Lush, intimate vegetation goes well with shabby-looking furnishings. Like guests at a party, the plants in this patio mingle with one another and lean over rustic chairs, joining the conversation.

a bit more elegance

Formal landscapes are typically symmetrical, with straight lines, geometric patterns, and near-perfect balance. Such landscapes can include neatly sheared hedges, topiaries, fountains, pools, or sculpture, and are always carefully maintained. For a more formal patio, aim for crisp, distinct lines. Cut stone and ceramic tile are stylish options. Brick and concrete pavers can look fairly dressy if installed neatly; mortared joints add more elegance. Edging should have a precise look—for example, very carefully installed pavers or invisible edging.

Overheads, planters, and other vertical elements of a formal patio are usually painted; if you will stain them, be sure to seal them well so they won't become discolored or peel. Coat paving materials with acrylic sealer to make them easier to clean.

A formal patio usually matches or consciously complements the architecture of the house. A traditional two-story brick or Tudor-style house calls for a basically rectangular brick patio. A flagstone patio will tie into a quaint bungalow as long as it is neatly installed. Vertical elements—benches, plant containers, or trellises—should repeat an architectural detail of the house, such as the trim around windows or the roof. Of course, the furniture you choose can be just as important visually as the patio itself (see pages 50–51 for furniture options).

◀ MODERN APPEAL

The bold geometric lines of this contemporary home are complemented by a fanciful privacy wall, Asian-style furnishings, and a raked gravel patio.

▶ TUSCAN STYLE

Like a stately Mediterranean café in the summer, the nearly white stone floors and dignified stone archway give a timeless appeal to this patio. The lush frame of flowers adds color and intensity.

▲ MARBLE DREAM

A carved marble-and-tile wall fountain in classic lines transports this patio to a faraway place and time. The capstones are a complementary limestone.

◀ NEATLY MANICURED

Meticulous landscaping, tailored patio furnishings, and a mortared stone surface with crisp joints and detail work give this patio a formal yet comfortable air.

planning for your needs

Most people want their outdoor space to serve a number of different purposes, such as entertaining, enjoying a quiet family meal, and reading a book. To add some versatility to your design, consider creating a little island of tranquility in an appealing section of your landscape—for instance, a small patio that floats a short distance away from the main deck/patio with a series of charming stepping-stones leading to it. The small private spaces often become the most treasured parts of a landscape.

It's important to have ample space for all the activities you consider important, as well as easy access to each part of the patio. See page 113 for how to plan cooking, dining, and lounging areas.

If your patio site receives lots of direct sunlight, you may want to choose lighter-colored materials, such as flagstone, since darker materials absorb and radiate the heat. An overhead structure can also help keep the patio cool and shady. Whichever materials you decide on, be sure they can handle the worst weather that comes your way, be it extremes of heat or cold.

Consider whether any new structures will affect the light coming into the house. For instance, an overhead structure that's attached to the house might block light to the kitchen or basement; if that's a concern, you might move the overhead slightly away from the house so that shafts of light will be able to filter through. If you're creating a new entry to the outdoors from your house, in effect you'll have a new hallway inside your home, and you may need to make some adjustments.

▶ *AN AMPLE RETREAT*

This space feels intimate enough for getting away from it all yet large enough for a friendly gathering of eight or so. The simplicity of the design and the respect for nature that shines through give this patio a contemplative quality.

▼ *TIMELESS APPEAL*

The weathered stone and timbers of this pergola resemble the remains of an ancient structure and form a generous frame for the rolling landscape. A flagstone patio provides plenty of space for dining and entertaining.

▲ ENGLISH GARDEN

This garden, lovingly tended and organized into neat areas, politely alternates with large stone slabs. A weathered bench is just right for having a cup of afternoon tea.

◄ JUNGLE THEME

Tropical bamboo provides the right amount of shade, and an inexpensive hammock is perfect for a jungle snooze.

Customize your outdoor space to suit the ways you like to entertain and socialize. Small children will use a smooth patio surface for trikes and toys with wheels, but many kid-friendly family activities—such as badminton, bocce ball, croquet, running through the sprinkler, and chasing lightning bugs—require plenty of lawn space. Think about where the young ones will congregate, then plan for easy sight lines so you can keep an eye on the kids while cooking or lounging.

You can place a patio most anywhere. In some cases, it makes sense to have one large patio and another smaller one. The most common patio is a rectangle in the backyard, attached to the house, but consider the other possibilities as well. A detached patio, joined to the house via a meandering path, offers a secluded retreat. A patio that wraps around two or more house walls can be accessed from two or more rooms. A side-yard patio (perhaps part of a wrap-around) can enable you to make good use of what is often wasted space. A large lot that has a slope can accommodate striking multilevel patios, joined by steps or walkways. If you live in an urban setting where space is tight, consider a side-yard patio or a rooftop patio, perhaps even a patio on top of a garage roof.

▲ **SUITED TO A SLOPE**
This secluded patio is carved out of a steep landscape, offering its visitors a view of the wooded hillside.

▼ **SMOOTH AS SILK**
A smooth surface is perfect for anything on wheels, and may become one of your children's favorite places to play.

▲ WRAPAROUND PATIO
Because both sides of this patio encircle the house, there is plenty of space for dining, entertaining, and gazing at the sweeping scenery.

▲ MAKING THE MOST OF A SIDE YARD
Often a side yard is wasted space, but a long, narrow space can be home to a memorable pathway. Here, a wall fountain and pool nestle right up against the neighbors' yard, leaving room for a paved path.

▶ SECLUDED RETREAT
A meandering path makes guests feel like they're on a treasure hunt as they make their way past an unusual fountain to a hidden dining area.

making the most of a small space

If the area outside your back door is small, don't despair. You have a wonderful opportunity to create a cozy, charming outdoor room with a lot of visual appeal.

One advantage of working with a small space is that a few artistic touches will pack a big visual wallop. For instance, four or five handmade, one-of-a-kind tiles set into a small patio will stand out; just a few decorative elements used for the edging will make it unique. And if your patio is small, you may be able to use more expensive materials since you won't need as much. Or you may be able to afford high-end products—for instance, hardwood duckboards or bluestone slabs—that install very easily.

With small spaces, it helps to think vertically. Upright elements such as arbors, trellises, and overheads allow you to add foliage and architectural detail without taking up much yard space. Attach a trellis to the house and allow climbing plants to create a wall of foliage.

Flower pots and planters allow you to increase the biodiversity of your setting for the cost of only a few square feet. Pots and some smaller planters can be arranged on shelves and stands to create a lush, colorful backdrop that also serves as a privacy screen.

When you're building in a small space, think about the best conversations you've had. Didn't most of them take place in a cozy spot—with just a couple of chairs and a table? Arrange furniture for maximum friendliness. Furniture that stows away adds versatility to a small outdoor room. With the addition of a few movable pieces, your restful retreat can be transformed into a lively entertainment space.

▼ *AN APPEALING MIX*
An eclectic group of pots, a chair, and a birdbath gather around a small pool. Adding various materials—here, limestone slabs and flagstones—makes the small space feel rich.

▼ AIRY YET SECLUDED

A tall bamboo fence and a few scattered potted plants add a feeling of privacy to this small gravel patio while preserving a sense of openness and space. A chaise lounge with a side table makes an admirable place to relax by yourself or with a close friend.

▲ VERSATILE OVERHEAD

A cheery coat of paint adds appeal to this overhead structure. The thin top slats provide partial shade while the heavier beams support large hanging plants.

▼ GROTTO

Dark colors are suited to a small shady spot. Here, a patio made of small stones and concrete chunks scattered amid dark plantless soil helps make the spot feel cool and comfortable.

▲ JUST ENOUGH SPACE

The patio in front of this bench is barely wider than a path, but leaves plenty of space for visitors to admire or tend to the surrounding foliage.

cooking and dining with flair

An outdoor cooking space can be a fairly simple affair—a grill unit and a small table in an area that has enough room for several people to converse while flipping burgers. Or it can be a full-blown kitchen complete with amenities such as a sink with running water, spacious counters and cabinets,

even a small refrigerator. In fact, including two cooking units in an outdoor kitchen design plus a pizza oven, a smoking chimney (for smoking meats), or a large deep-fat cooker (for frying a turkey) has become increasingly popular, and for good reason: it makes sense to move the messiest and smokiest cooking operations

out of the house, where they are fun rather than an annoyance. Some families enjoy having a second gas-powered grill unit with a tight-fitting lid that can keep cooked food warm. See pages 82–87 for more details.

Before starting to design, learn where the sun will shine during the hours when you are most likely to cook. Place the outdoor kitchen in a comfortable spot, so that you'll have plenty of shade during late afternoons in summer. If a tree is not nearby to provide shade, perhaps install a large umbrella. Plan the cooking area so that you have easy access to the kitchen—it should be near the kitchen door but 4 or 5 feet off to the side, out of the main traffic pattern. The outdoor dining area should be nearby.

Check the manufacturer's guidelines for safe placement of your cooking unit. It should not be near anything flammable— for instance, a wood railing. All food preparation areas should be made from materials that are easy to clean; ceramic tile is ideal. Make sure that food won't touch pressure-treated lumber at any time, because the chemicals that treat the lumber can contaminate the food.

◄ *AN INVITING OUTDOOR ROOM*
A waffle-like overhead gently encloses
this outdoor kitchen and dining area.
The chandelier is made for outdoor use.
A stone floor with mortared joints is easily
cleaned with a garden hose.

▲ GRILLING WITH STYLE

Setting the grill away from the house keeps the smoke and mess of cooking away from the seating and traffic areas. This grill is built into a low stone wall that defines the patio area and permits a pleasant view of the rest of the yard.

▶ FULL-SERVICE KITCHEN

This outdoor kitchen can handle just about any cooking assignment. It features a sink, plenty of counter space, a grill, a side burner, and a pizza oven. All are housed in a stone-faced counter with a granite slab countertop.

◀ EXOTIC APPEAL

An opulent pool with a tropical waterfall sets the tone for this luxurious dining area. Eating a meal in a setting like this makes you feel like you're on a vacation.

GATHERING SPOTS

There's no one layout that is best for a party. Your friends may like to congregate in a large group, in which case you will want a generous patio surface—ideally, with at least 15 square feet per person. If partygoers like to dance outdoors, install a fairly smooth surface, such as a paver patio, and plan how you will set speakers outdoors or in a window. Many people prefer to socialize in groups of three or four yet don't want to be shut off from the rest of the party. Deep stairs, a small patio area off the deck, or a walkway through the foliage can be ideal for these friends.

Be sure your guests are comfortable. Provide lighting at night and shade during the afternoon. If you have friends or family members in wheelchairs or on crutches, build ramps or other alternatives to steps and make sure all the surfaces are level and smooth.

▲ AN OUTDOOR LIVING ROOM

The blazing fire in this generous fireplace sets the whole patio aglow with welcoming warmth sure to lure guests. The comfortable seating area resembles an indoor living room.

◄ PARTY LIGHTS

Mason jars shining with candlelight hang from an overhead, providing a festive atmosphere for outdoor entertaining. A low-voltage outdoor chandelier further illuminates the dining area.

▶ LODGE SETTING

This outdoor room has all the comforts of the indoors. The roof offers protection from the rain, allowing use of indoor furniture. A blazing fireplace provides a comfortable dining experience even when the weather is cool.

▲ AN ARTISTIC TOUCH

Two separate patio areas linked with a curving path add versatility to a landscape. Here, the stone path winds around a millstone fountain, which serves as a distant focal point for the shaded lounging area.

▶ HOLE IN ONE

A putting green adjacent to this patio invites friendly competition at parties. Other crowd-pleasing backyard games include bocce ball, croquet, and horseshoes.

covering up

The idea behind a patio is to have a place to be out in the natural world. But sometimes Mother Nature can get mean, and at those times we often want to watch nature, not be out in it. Fortunately, there are a number of products that will shelter you from bugs and bad weather while letting you breathe free.

AWNINGS

There are awnings to fit every home. Extended, they protect you, but they can also retract against your house so that you can enjoy full sun whenever you like. You'll find plenty of sizes and cheery fabrics from which to choose.

Awnings project from the house about 10 feet and are available in a variety of widths, up to about 20 feet. If you want to install them under eaves or an overhang, they can generally be hung as low as 7 feet.

MOTORIZED OR MANUAL Motorized awnings offer the most convenience because they open and close with just the touch of a button (remote controls are also available). An electric motor hides inside the awning structure with a cord that plugs into an electric outlet. A motorized awning typically mounts on a wall but can also be installed on a soffit or an overhang.

Manually operated awnings are opened and closed with a simple hand crank. Look for an awning that operates smoothly and quietly and is not too difficult to crank. Manual models have support arms that can be positioned vertically on the patio floor or angled back against your house wall. They also have floor and wall mounting plates.

AWNING WALLS Sun-blocking panels that extend down 5 feet or so can be attached to an awning. Some, like blinds, are designed to partially block sun and wind while letting in air and light. Others, like shades, block all of the sun's glare. These need to be anchored from the bottom as well as from the top.

◄ STYLISH OVERHEAD

Retractable canopies hang from a pergola, providing additional protection from the sun. Canopy fabrics come in a variety of widths and colors.

▼ **ADDING SIDE SHADE**

Pull-down awnings operate like large window shades to bring privacy as well as comfort to a patio.

Some awning companies offer an attachable net that creates a bug-free screened-in room. Side zippers provide easy access. This option is more flexible and less expensive than creating a true screened-in room.

SCREENED RETREATS

A screened room not only protects you from mosquitoes; it also protects you from the rain and provides filtered shade on hot days. Kids will build memories when they have a sleepover in a screened room in the middle of summer. A screened room is often attached to the house and is rectangular in shape. But you can also buy a gazebo kit that comes equipped with screens. See pages 46–49 for instructions on building screened rooms.

▲ **PUSH-BUTTON AWNING**

Noontime shadows clearly show how cool and shady it is beneath this retractable awning, which extends out 10 feet from the house with just the push of a button.

▲ **LIGHTING UP THE NIGHT**

A string of globed lights imparts a festive feel—or perhaps a romantic glow—to this outdoor dining area.

▶ **A REFUGE FROM PESTS**

A screened gazebo is a welcome retreat any time, but especially at twilight, when bugs become a nuisance. It's a great way to house tables of food at a party, to ward off flies and other pests.

waterworks

Water seems to have a natural affinity for stones, bricks, and tile; they always look at home in each other's company. So it makes sense to add a pond or fountain near or in the middle of a patio.

PONDS

A backyard pond within view of the patio can become a tranquil and scenic focal point as well as a good source of water for birds and butterflies, or frogs and fish. Even a small pond is a natural magnet for wildlife.

If you'd like to go really small, a variety of containers can be used; for instance, a barrel, a tub, or a water bowl. Small containers can be placed right on the patio. There are a number of tub kits available that require only water, a pump, and some plants. (See pages 70–71 for instructions.)

A pond with a waterfall is not as difficult to install as you may think. You will need to lay down

▲ **PORTABLE POND**
A container pond, like a potted plant, adds its charm wherever you need it—in this case, a ledge along the perimeter of the garden.

◄ **TABLE-SIDE POND**
A large, elegant pond is spacious enough for a variety of water plants and fish. Here, it provides a tranquil backdrop for the adjacent eating area.

a liner along the waterfall path as well as in the pond. A pump will keep water circulating from the pond to the waterfall and back again. The pump can be turned on and off manually or controlled by a timer.

FOUNTAINS

Many people find the sight or sound of bubbling or cascading water peaceful and relaxing. You'll find fountains in all shapes and sizes to suit any budget. Some are classic in design while others add touches of whimsy, such as a statuette of an angel or a frog. No matter what your preference,

a fountain in or near your patio is sure to become a focal point as well as inviting to birds and other wildlife. See pages 68–69 for instructions on making a small container fountain.

If you live in an area with freezing temperatures, avoid concrete and ceramic fountains because they will be prone to crack and break. Bronze withstands all weather conditions and ages well. Aerators and spitters keep the water looking clear.

▲ BACKYARD SPRING
With water cascading down several layers of flagstone, this pond looks like a natural backyard spring rather than a man-made pool. A hidden pump quietly circulates water up to the top of the cascade.

◄ THE MAGIC OF FLOWING WATER
Water flowing downward from this garden wall adds an element of gentle sound and movement to the landscape. A simple pump with tubing keeps the water moving.

Fountains can be roughly divided into two types: those that spray and those that spill. Spray fountains shoot water upward in various patterns. Spray fountains can add movement and interest to your pond while aerating the water and providing oxygen to plants and fish. Some models operate on solar power; they feature an integral low-voltage pump, a filter, and a thin solar-energy panel.

▲ *OVERFLOWING WITH APPEAL*
A tulip-shaped spurt of water seems to emanate from a mythological sea creature beneath the surface, adding a whimsical note to this cheerful pond.

Spill fountains sit above or adjacent to a pond or catch basin, sending streams of water into it. A garden fountain, perhaps with several tiers, usually comes with a self-contained water basin and a pump to recirculate the water, and does not require a special plumbing hookup. All you need to do is fill the fountain with water and plug it in. The water sound varies from loud to soft, depending on the type of fountain. Wall fountains work on the same principle: water recirculates from a pool or container through plastic tubing to the outlet.

▲ *HOMEMADE CHARM*
Adding a fountain to your patio can be as simple as plugging in a pump and running tubing into a tilted pot. This ingenious setup creates an interesting focal point along a garden wall.

▶ *TOUCH OF CLASS*
A well-placed fountain with simple, classic lines adds an artistic dimension to this patio.

gardening with style

You can't have a beautiful patio without stunning foliage. Don't treat plants as an afterthought; be sure to incorporate them into your plans from the beginning.

CREATING A FRAME AND AN OUTLOOK

Plants should form the backdrop for a patio and its activities, not encroach on its space. The best strategy is usually to place short plants next to the patio and progressively taller plants behind them. You can also place plants in pots or planters in the middle of the patio to function as frames, defining different areas of the space.

Also orient the patio to suit your plants. If you have a wonderful tree, a pretty expanse of lawn, or flower beds that you like to show off, be sure to shape the patio so that people sitting on it will naturally face the view. Avoid having seating that makes people turn their backs on the yard and face the house.

▼ *ENHANCING THE VIEW*
An array of low-lying potted plants brings a garden of flowers into the seating area on this patio while leaving the view open to larger plantings in the distance.

◀ *A GALLERY OF FOLIAGE*
The view from this patio is gratifyingly lush. Placing lower plants in front and taller plants in the back creates a lush and colorful effect.

ADDING FLOWERS

You can add a splash of color to your patio inexpensively with a bit of creativity and time. Flower boxes can be purchased fairly cheap; if you find some old ones at a garage sale, you can spruce them up with a quick coat of paint. Place the boxes along the perimeter of the patio or on any nearby steps. Hang flower baskets from an overhead or from the soffit beside the doorway.

If you have enough room and enough sun in a corner of your patio, consider adding a raised garden. A small cedar or masonry bed that is waist high is perfect for growing cooking herbs as well as flowers.

To keep the plants well watered with little effort, install a micro-sprinkler system; pages 63–65 show how.

▲ *AN ISLAND ESCAPE*
Set on a pedestal, this remote eating area is neatly framed by a low stone wall and an inside border of hearty flowering plants.

▼ *FOLIAGE THAT FLOWS*
Flowers that spill over the edge of a pot add dramatic color at several levels to this charming gated patio.

ADDING VERTICAL COLOR

If space is tight, it often makes sense to add foliage by building up. Place a trellis in a sunny spot against the house or against nearby fencing. Choose a climbing plant such as dark purple clematis, which is very hearty and will grow quickly and bloom with fragrant flowers. You can either buy a trellis or make one fairly easily with scraps of wood.

ATTRACTING BIRDS AND BUTTERFLIES

If you'd like to attract birds, butterflies, and hummingbirds, include some plants that they like. For hummingbirds, add flowers such as hibiscus and fuchsia, which have bright colors, rich nectar, and a tubular shape. Be careful not to use poisonous chemicals or insecticides for weed or pest control in your flower beds or pots. These will either sicken or kill hummers as well as butterflies and their caterpillars and larvae.

▲ AN ENTRANCE WITH FLAIR
A trellis heavy with flowery foliage offers a romantic entrance to this simple brick patio dotted with clay pots.

INCLUDING EDIBLES

A vegetable garden need not be homely. As long as you frame the garden area attractively, perhaps with a grid of pavers or a series of raised beds, even the humblest of greens and the bushiest of tomato plants will look surprisingly attractive.

▲ ADDING A WALL OF COLOR
If space is tight, building upward with foliage along a sunny patio wall maximizes color while using minimal space. Many sturdy climbing plants grow quickly with a simple homemade trellis to grab onto.

▶ EDIBLE APPEAL
This garden, bursting with a variety of edible plants, is a pleasure to survey. Flower beds surround a simple stone birdbath—a layout that is sure to attract birds and butterflies as well as people.

storage options

There's no reason to have a patio cluttered with hoses, bags of charcoal, or garden tools. With a little planning and a judicious purchase or two, you can keep all of that stuff in attractive storage units.

Store your hose in style. There are several options: a hose bowl has a side hole that lets you leave the hose connected to the faucet and can resemble terra cotta or granite (though it's really polyethylene). A hose cart can store 200 feet of hose and lets you wheel it where you need it;

▲ **ATTRACTIVE HOSE HOUSING**
A ceramic hose pot with a shiny blue glaze keeps the garden hose handy and eliminates the eyesore.

▶ **DOUBLE DUTY**
A simple storage bench can hide a good number of tools and implements. Add a cushion or two, and you also have a pleasing place to sit.

the hose will last longer because it will get handled and stepped on less often.

A storage chest or bench is a popular storage solution for patios. It lets you add seating to your patio while keeping tools and watering accessories out of sight yet close at hand. You can also store cushions, pool toys, and lawn games in a bench. See pages 52–53 for instructions on building a wooden bench with storage space.

It's easy to keep your garden tools neat and organized when you hang them on a metal tool rack. Such racks are good for long-handled shovels, forks and spades, and hand tools; some models hold up to 16 tools. Mount the rack in your garden shed or on a protected outside wall.

If you have a lot of stuff to store—long-handled yard tools such as rakes, shovels, and weed trimmers; a mower; planter pots; and outdoor furniture cushions—you may want a storage shed. Type "storage shed" into a search engine and you'll be given a number of companies that sell storage sheds so attractive that they may become features of your patio. Some models include flower boxes and shutters.

▲ FARMHOUSE TOUCH

This lattice-backed potting bench has farmhouse appeal, making pots and shovels seem like decorative elements. It's also a practical storage solution for a corner of the patio.

▼ COTTAGE CHARM

Complete with window boxes and a shingled roof, this storage shed, built from a kit, looks as though it materialized from the pages of a storybook.

▲ STYLISH STORAGE

Wood sheds have replaced the tin ones of yesteryear. This tall, narrow shed offers plenty of storage capacity in a compact space and will last for years when the wood is properly sealed.

◀ **CENTER OF ATTENTION**

A large gas-fueled firepit has a wide ledge for seating, making it a great gathering spot on cool evenings.

▼ **PORTABLE WARMTH**

A propane heater, with the tank at the base and an infrared heating element at the top, resembles a floor lamp. It requires no hookup, and some models come with wheels so you can bring the heat where you need it.

getting comfortable

Spending time outdoors often means contending with heat, cold, and bugs. While you don't want to make the outdoors feel just like the indoors, there are products available to make you much more comfortable.

HEATERS

To keep the party going when the weather turns cool, use a portable stand-up patio heater. This type of heater hooks up to propane or natural gas and produces a circle of heat as large as 20 feet in diameter. Or choose an overhead infrared heater, which directs heat down to warm a more defined area.

For a more low-tech solution, consider an inexpensive outdoor wood-burning fireplace. Old-fashioned-looking models are made of cast iron or clay; modern-looking versions are generally made of powder-finished steel.

▲ **INSTANT OVERHEAD HEAT**

Overhead infrared lights provide near-instantaneous warmth for a modest electrical output. Many units can be simply hooked onto an overhead structure and plugged into a standard electrical outlet.

▲ A REFRESHING MIST

A patio misting system that attaches to an overhead structure is simple to install and inexpensive. In this arrangement, guests can choose their seat depending on how much mist they desire.

MISTERS

If you live in an area with hot, dry summers, consider installing an outdoor misting system, which sprays a fine mist that cools and refreshes. Type "patio mister" into a search engine to find several companies that make misting systems that are modestly priced and easy to install.

One option is a kit that includes at least 20 feet of hose and 10 to 15 nozzles that can attach to an overhead structure to generate a gentle spray over a large area. Or you can purchase a fan that attaches to a garden hose and directs a heavier mist at a more defined area.

DEBUGGING STRATEGIES

Here, from the Environmental Protection Agency, are tips for keeping mosquitoes from biting you and your family:

- Because mosquito larvae need water to grow to adulthood, be on the lookout for little places where water can collect in your yard: old tires, buckets, plastic covers, toys, etc. Fill temporary pools with dirt. Make sure rain gutters are unclogged.
- Spraying the yard can be an effective temporary solution. Spray during peak periods of mosquito flight, often around dusk. A very short-lived (pyrethroid) insecticide is often used for this purpose; it usually breaks down within a couple of hours following application, particularly in sunlight. The downside is that the spray can damage populations of desirable insects and contaminate garden crops.
- The single most effective deterrent is to apply a repellent that contains DEET to your skin; no other product comes close in effectiveness.
- There is no good evidence that citronella candles keep mosquitoes from biting. However, there are some health concerns associated with inhalation of smoke from chemical candles.
- "Bug zappers" are ineffective in reducing mosquito biting rates and kill many harmless or beneficial insects. Sonic repellers are also ineffective.

making the
most of your patio

A patio is really just an outdoor floor. To feel more like an inviting room, it needs vertical elements to complete it. The right finishing touches and amenities, such as overheads, furniture, plants, water features, and even outdoor kitchens, can turn your patio into a welcoming retreat.

patio overheads

In addition to providing shade, an overhead structure (sometimes called a pergola or lanai) functions as a "space frame" that defines all or part of your patio. It may also provide a place for plants to climb or a ceiling from which to hang planters.

Choose a design that harmonizes with your home and your patio. An overhead need not be built from the same materials as your house, but the new materials should not contrast jarringly. A formal setting probably calls for neatly spaced members and several coats of paint, and a more informal home may work best with an unpainted overhead with a few fanciful elements.

When considering an overhead structure, check the sight lines from the house and from the patio. Make sure the new overhead will not make a room too dark or inhibit a pleasing view.

HOW IT'S PUT TOGETHER

An overhead can be freestanding or attached to the house at one end with a ledger, as shown below. Posts can be set deep in holes for added lateral strength or rest on post anchors that are attached to the patio. A beam or two can rest on top of the posts or be attached to the side of the posts, as shown. Rafters can be set on top of two beams or tie into a ledger at one end. Top pieces, sometimes called lath, are usually evenly spaced and sized to provide the right amount of shade.

Use lumber that will resist rotting and warping. Pressure-treated lumber is the most rot resistant; the dark heartwood of redwood or cedar also resists rot and is better looking.

RAFTER AND BEAM SPANS

If rafters or beams span too long a distance, they will sag in time. (A rafter span is the distance from beam to beam or from beam to ledger; a beam span is the distance from post to post.) The following are some recommended maximum spans.

RAFTER SIZE	IF RAFTERS ARE SPACED	
	16" APART	24" APART
2 × 4	9'	8'
2 × 6	14'	12'
2 × 8	18'	16'

BEAM SIZE	IF BEAMS ARE SPACED	
	12' APART	16' APART
2 × 8	8'	6'
2 × 10	10'	8'
4 × 6	8'	6'
4 × 8	12'	10'
4 × 10	14'	12'

Note: A doubled 2-by beam has the same strength as a 4-by beam. For instance, a beam made with two 2 by 6s is equivalent to one 4 by 6.

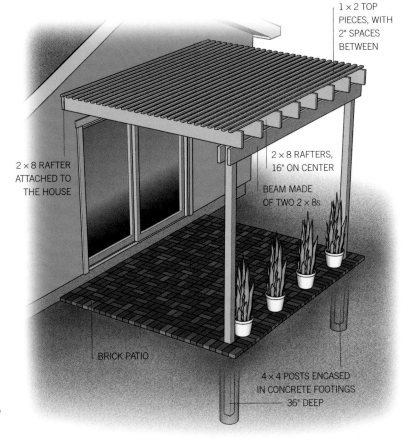

1 × 2 TOP PIECES, WITH 2" SPACES BETWEEN

2 × 8 RAFTER ATTACHED TO THE HOUSE

2 × 8 RAFTERS, 16" ON CENTER

BEAM MADE OF TWO 2 × 8s

BRICK PATIO

4 × 4 POSTS ENCASED IN CONCRETE FOOTINGS 36" DEEP

CHOOSING THE COVERING

Overheads are most commonly topped with 1 by 2s, 2 by 2s, or other small-dimensioned lumber. But there are other options. Shade cloths are available in a variety of densities to provide from 20 to 90 percent shade. Lattice panels can be installed quickly, provide fairly even shade throughout the day, and add a richly textured look. Be sure to support lattice every 16 inches or it will sag. Other options include woven reed or bamboo shades, which can be rolled up when shade is not desired.

SHADE POSSIBILITIES

Shade needs vary according to the time of day and the time of year, so spend some time developing a shade plan. If you want midday shade, run the top pieces of your overhead east to west; for

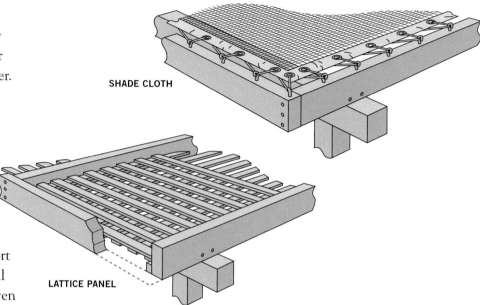

SHADE CLOTH

LATTICE PANEL

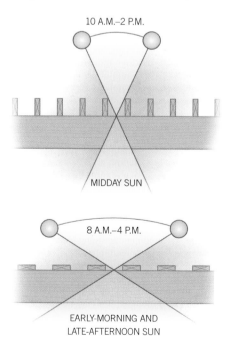

10 A.M.–2 P.M.

MIDDAY SUN

8 A.M.–4 P.M.

EARLY-MORNING AND
LATE-AFTERNOON SUN

more shade in the morning and early evening, run the pieces north to south. (Of course, changing the orientation of the top pieces means changing the orientation of the beams and rafters as well.)

Experiment with different materials and configurations by temporarily screwing some pieces on top of the rafters. Pay attention to the amount of shade they provide in both the morning and the afternoon.

Top pieces laid on edge diffuse early-morning and late-afternoon sun but let in plenty of light at midday. The same pieces laid flat admit more sun in the early morning and late afternoon but block midday sun.

DRESSING IT UP

Rafter and beam ends that overhang a structure are highly visible, so you may want to cut them to achieve a decorative

pattern. Experiment with designs, using a compass if the design calls for a curve or two. Once you've settled on a design, make a cardboard or plywood template, use it to trace the pattern onto the rafter or beam ends, then cut with a jigsaw.

You can also dress up post tops. The easiest way is to buy decorative post caps that screw in. Or, use a circular saw to cut a series of shallow bands and perhaps to make chamfer cuts on the tops.

ATTACHING A LEDGER

If the overhead is attached to the house, begin construction by installing a ledger. The ledger is typically made of the same dimension lumber as the rafters. A ledger must be firmly attached with long screws that reach into the house's framing, not just the siding and sheathing.

On a one-story house, it is often best to attach the ledger

just below the eaves. On a two-story house, you can usually tie into a band joist (also called a rim joist) located between the floors, as shown (see right). Find the band joist by measuring down from a second-story window.

A ledger can be attached in several ways, depending on the type of siding you have and the local building codes. Avoid creating a joint where water will collect and cause rot. Some builders prefer to cut out a section of siding, slip in metal flashing, and tuck the ledger under the flashing. However, simpler arrangements, such as those that follow, work just as well.

If you have beveled horizontal siding, then use an inverted piece of siding as shown (see above) to create a plumb surface for attaching the ledger. If your siding is not beveled, you can simply screw the ledger tight to it. Or, use the hold-back method (see sideview illustration). Slip three or four stainless-steel washers between the ledger and the siding when driving each screw. This will allow water to flow behind the ledger. To tie into a brick wall, use masonry screws or screws with lag shields.

BUILDING A BASIC OVERHEAD

Following are the basic steps for building an overhead. If the posts will sit on top of a reasonably level (or consistently sloped) patio, cut all the posts to the same length. Otherwise, install

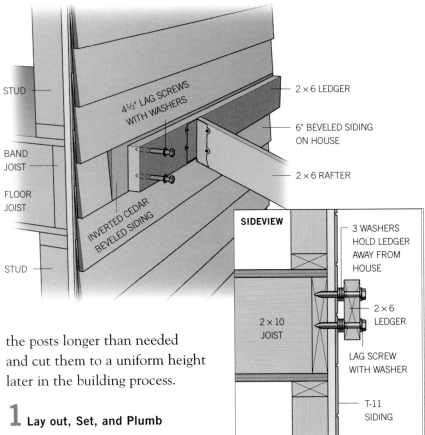

STUD

BAND JOIST

FLOOR JOIST

STUD

4½" LAG SCREWS WITH WASHERS

INVERTED CEDAR BEVELED SIDING

2 × 6 LEDGER

6" BEVELED SIDING ON HOUSE

2 × 6 RAFTER

SIDEVIEW

2 × 10 JOIST

3 WASHERS HOLD LEDGER AWAY FROM HOUSE

2 × 6 LEDGER

LAG SCREW WITH WASHER

T-11 SIDING

the posts longer than needed and cut them to a uniform height later in the building process.

1 Lay out, Set, and Plumb the Posts

Use batter boards and lines to establish the correct locations of the posts, and check your layout for square (see pages 135–37). Posts may be set on top of the patio using post anchors that elevate them slightly; this is usually the best choice if you have a concrete patio. To install a post

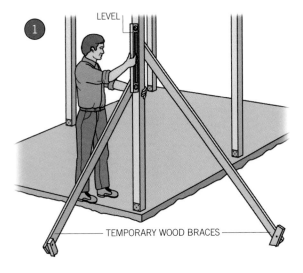

LEVEL

TEMPORARY WOOD BRACES

anchor, drill holes using a masonry bit and drive masonry screws.

Setting posts in post holes provides additional lateral strength. If your patio is made of pavers laid in sand, remove some of them and dig holes for the posts; you'll need to cut pavers to fit around the posts later. Or, dig post holes just beyond the patio.

Plumb each post in both directions. Secure each post with temporary wood braces nailed to wood stakes driven into the ground or to heavy weights resting on the patio.

2 Install the Beam(s)

If you have a ledger, the top of the beam should be at the same height as the bottom of the ledger. A beam should overhang the posts by at least a few inches on each side. To install a solid beam on top of the posts, work with two or more helpers. Cut the posts to the same height. Attach a post cap to the top of each post, slip the beam into the caps, and drive deck screws or nails to attach. If you do not like the look of post caps, set the beam directly on top of the posts, drill angled pilot holes, and drive screws to attach the beam to the posts.

ANOTHER BEAM OPTION You can also build a beam using two pieces of 2-by lumber attached to either side of the post. Use a square to draw lines around the post to mark the exact height of the beam on both sides. Attach the two pieces with deck screws or nails, or drill holes and install bolts that go all the way through all three pieces. With this type of beam, you can install 4-by-4 bracing as shown.

3 Add Rafters and Braces

On top of the beams and/or on the side of the ledger, mark for evenly spaced rafters. Cut rafters to overhang the beam by at least a few inches. Attach the rafters by drilling angled pilot holes and driving screws or nails, or use a rafter tie, as shown. To make the structure more stable, nail or screw 2-by-4 or 2-by-6 braces between the beams and posts. The braces should be at least 3 feet long, with the ends cut at 45 degrees.

4 Cover Top Pieces

Top the structure with 1 by 2s or other small-dimensioned lumber, spaced to achieve the desired amount of shade (see page 40). One common method is to "self-space" the top pieces: use a scrap of the lumber as a spacing guide.

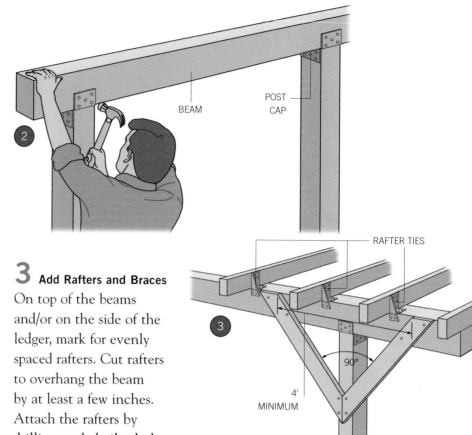

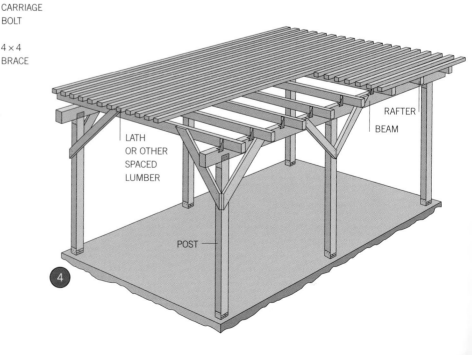

simple freestanding overhead

A modest-sized overhead like this can enclose a small patio, as shown, or define a portion of a larger patio. The overhead can be built larger as long as you follow the guidelines for rafter and beam spans given on page 39.

DESIGN ELEMENTS

The crisscrossed pattern of on-end 2 by 4s provides a fair amount of shade in the morning and evening and less during midday. If you want more or different coverage, space the 2-by-4 top pieces closer together, or install another type of covering, such as closely spaced 1 by 2s or lattice panels (see page 40).

Posts made of pressure-treated 4 by 4s are ideal for durability (especially below grade) but often develop cracks that do not affect strength but are unsightly, particularly when the wood is painted. Wrapping posts in 1-by fascia boards solves the problem and adds subtle texture. The fascia also provides a ledge for the 2-by-8 beams to rest on, eliminating the need for bolts.

Use lumber proven to resist rot in your locale. Pressure-treated lumber is the best choice if the structure will be painted, or choose dark heartwood of redwood or cedar if the structure will be stained. To further ensure against deterioration, soak all board ends in sealer before you install the boards. If you intend to paint the structure, also prime all the pieces before installing them.

TWO DESIGN DETAILS

To wrap a 4-by-4 post with 1-by fascia, you have two options. Use the dimensions shown to cut the pieces slightly wider than the post; this will compensate for the inevitable imperfections in the lumber.

You can quickly draw a classic ogee pattern for the rafter ends on a cardboard or plywood template using a square and a compass.

TWO WAYS TO WRAP A 4 × 4 WITH 1×

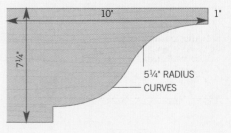

OGEE RAFTER END CUT FOR A 2 × 8

43

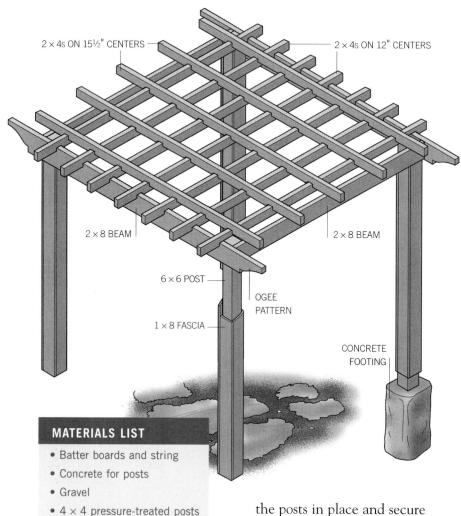

2 × 4s ON 15½" CENTERS

2 × 4s ON 12" CENTERS

2 × 8 BEAM

2 × 8 BEAM

6 × 6 POST

OGEE
PATTERN

1 × 8 FASCIA

CONCRETE
FOOTING

MATERIALS LIST

- Batter boards and string
- Concrete for posts
- Gravel
- 4 × 4 pressure-treated posts
- 2 × 8 beams
- 2 × 4s for top crosspieces
- 1 × 6 and perhaps
  1 × 4 fascia to wrap posts
- Galvanized nails and
  deck screws
- Wood sealer
- Primer and acrylic-latex
  paint, or stain

SET THE POSTS

Lay out the post locations using batter boards and string (see pages 135–36). Dig holes for the footings at least 36 inches deep and put about 3 inches of gravel at the bottom of each hole. Set the posts in place and secure them so that they are plumb in both directions, supporting them with two temporary braces attached to stakes driven into the ground (see pages 41–42). You will cut the posts to height later.

Check that the posts are square to each other as well as equidistant from each other; you will likely need to make minor adjustments. Mix and pour concrete into each hole. Wait a day for the concrete to set.

Using a level set atop an 8-foot-long straight board, mark the tops of the posts level with each other, at least 8 feet above the ground. Use a square to draw a line around each post; cut with a circular saw.

CUT AND ATTACH THE BEAMS

Cut the two side beams to run from post to post and attach them flush with the post tops using nails or screws.

Cut the two long beams, using the ogee pattern on page 43 or another pattern. Make sure the beams are long enough to over-hang attractively. Attach the long beams.

Mark the tops of all the beams for the 2-by-4 rafters, 12 inches on center.

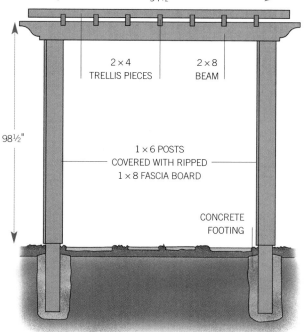

94½"

2 × 4
TRELLIS PIECES

2 × 8
BEAM

98½"

1 × 6 POSTS
COVERED WITH RIPPED
1 × 8 FASCIA BOARD

CONCRETE
FOOTING

WRAP THE POSTS

For each post, cut four fascia boards using one of the patterns shown on page 43. The bottom of each fascia board should be about 1 inch above the concrete. Two of the fascia boards butt up to the underside of the beams and two run to the top of the post. You will need to cut a notch in at least one of the boards. Nail or screw the fascia pieces to the posts.

NOTCH AND INSTALL THE 2 BY 4s

Cut the 2-by-4 rafters (the lower pieces) to length, overhanging the beams by 6 inches on either side. Lay one rafter across the long beams, center it for an equal overhang at both ends, and mark for 1½-inch-wide notches where the rafter crosses the beams. Gang-cut the notches as shown (below right). Install the rafters by drilling pilot holes and driving screws or nails.

Cut the 2-by-4 top pieces to length so that they overhang the side beams by 6 inches on either side. (If the posts were laid out accurately, the top 2 by 4s will be the same length as the 2-by-4 rafters.) Lay one top piece in place, mark it for notches, and cut the notches (seven notches per board) as you did for the rafters. Drill pilot holes and drive screws or nails to attach the top 2 by 4s to the rafters.

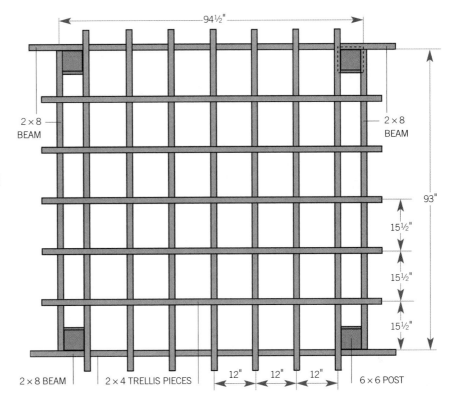

FINISH

Sand the fascia and round the corners to eliminate any splinters. Touch up the primer as needed and top-coat the entire structure with acrylic-latex paint. Or, apply stain and finish.

GANG-CUTTING NOTCHES

To quickly and accurately cut notches, cut all the boards to length and clamp them together with their ends flush. Use a square and a scrap of 2-by material to draw lines for notches that will fit snugly over a rafter or beam. Set a circular saw to the correct depth (1½ inches) and test-cut a scrap to be sure the setting is correct. First cut the outside lines, then make a series of closely spaced cuts in the inside of the notch. Use a hammer and chisel to clean out and square up the notches.

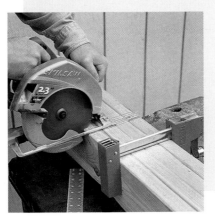

screened room and sunroom kits

A tightly screened-in patio keeps out mosquitoes, shelters you from rain, and lengthens the yearly period when you can enjoy your yard. A sunroom can make your patio comfortable all year round.

If you type "patio sunroom" or "patio screened room" into a Web search engine, you will find companies that sell a wide variety of covers for a patio. Some screened enclosures are tentlike structures that can be erected or dismantled in a few hours. Permanent screened rooms or sunrooms may be made of wood components, but most are made with aluminum frames.

To make sure your enclosure is durable, check that the company you're buying from has been in business for a number of years, offers a solid guarantee, and has people you can ask questions of over the phone. Be sure that the kit will arrive with complete installation instructions; the company should also provide clear directions on how to measure your house and patio.

Take time to learn about the screen and/or storm window panels. (If the literature does not provide enough information, talk to a salesperson at the company.) Frames, which are typically vinyl, should be strong; cheap frames tend to come apart at the corners. The rubber gaskets should seal tightly and the latch system should be strong and durable. Panels should be easy to remove yet seal tightly. Make sure you can buy replacement parts in the future.

Kits are designed for homeowner installation and come with all the parts you need. Once the ledger and bottom plates have been attached, most of the pieces snap together or join by driving a screw or two. You will need at least one sturdy ladder and one able helper.

Left, above: *Self-storing windows clamp tightly to the frame, yet are easily removed without the use of tools.* **Left, below:** *You can open and close pleated shades to control light, heat, and save energy on a year-round basis. They provide shade in the summer and act as blankets in the winter.*

AWNINGS

If you want shade only from time to time, consider installing an awning. You open and close it by turning a crank, or you can spend a bit more for a motorized unit. Awning fabric is typically made of several layers of different materials. Look for at least a five-year guarantee against deterioration and color fading.

Aluminum or vinyl-coated fiberglass screening comes in either black or gray. For serious glare protection, see if you can order solar screening made from tightly woven vinyl-covered fiberglass. Aluminum and bronze solar screening is very expensive. Pet-resistant screening made of vinyl-coated polyester that's heavier and much stronger than normal screening is also available.

Most kit windows are glazed with acrylic rather than glass. Acrylic is lighter than glass, making it a good choice especially for windows more than 42 inches wide. Acrylic scratches easily,

however, so be sure to get a scratch-resistant coating.

The enclosure will attach either to the house's siding or to an overhanging eave. The base of the framing typically attaches to a patio with masonry screws, which are not difficult to drive. In most cases, two people can assemble and attach a metal-framed sunroom in a day or two.

To keep a sunroom from overheating in the summer, buy reflective shades, which can block nearly all the sun's heat. To keep the room warm in the winter, consider winter "blankets" that both increase solar heat and insulate against heat loss.

wood-framed screened rooms

If you have basic carpentry framing skills, it won't be too difficult to build an attached screened-in room from wood. Since the studs and rafters support only screens and a lightweight roof, they do not need to be nearly as substantial as standard framing.

FRAMING THE ROOM

The 2-by-4 studs can be spaced up to 4 feet apart. The rafters must fall directly over the studs or the top plate will sag. Fiberglass roof panels must be supported every 4 feet with special contoured support moldings that you can buy along with the panels. Build the outside wall shorter than the ledger's height so that the roof slopes at least 1 foot for every 10 running feet.

Plan for the project's footprint to fall at least 4 inches inside the patio's perimeter. The patio should be solidly constructed; a 4-inch-thick concrete slab will do fine, as will sand-laid pavers as long as they are installed on a solid gravel and sand bed (see Chapter 5). Buy the screen door before you build, and size the opening to fit it.

Use pressure-treated lumber and prime all pieces before you install them. At the house, install a ledger (see page 41). Build the outer wall and use a circular saw to cut ¼-inch "scuppers" (grooves) every 3 feet or so in the bottom edges of the sills to allow for drainage. Hold the framing plumb with temporary braces and attach the bottom sill plate using masonry screws. Add 4-by-4 corner posts and build the side walls.

Cut 2-by-6 rafters so that they overhang about a foot and attach them to

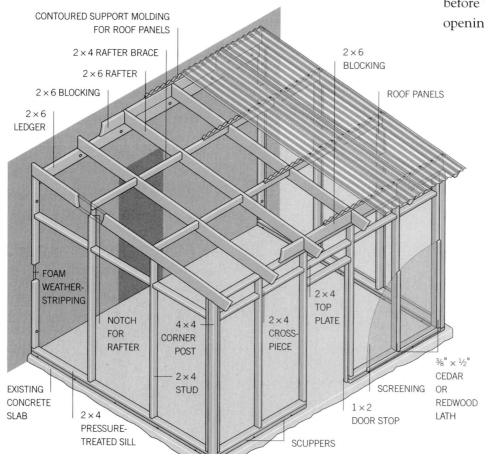

CONTOURED SUPPORT MOLDING FOR ROOF PANELS

2 × 4 RAFTER BRACE

2 × 6 RAFTER

2 × 6 BLOCKING

2 × 6 LEDGER

2 × 6 BLOCKING

ROOF PANELS

FOAM WEATHER-STRIPPING

NOTCH FOR RAFTER

4 × 4 CORNER POST

2 × 4 CROSS-PIECE

2 × 4 TOP PLATE

2 × 4 STUD

3/8" × 1/2" CEDAR OR REDWOOD LATH

SCREENING

1 × 2 DOOR STOP

EXISTING CONCRETE SLAB

2 × 4 PRESSURE-TREATED SILL

SCUPPERS

the ledger and to the top plate of the outer wall. Install 2-by-6 crosspieces every 4 feet between the rafters, attach the contoured support moldings, and install the fiberglass panels using special screws with self-sealing washers.

To make a frame for the screens, attach 1-by-2 stops flush with the outside edges of the frames.

MAKING WOOD-FRAMED SCREENS

1 Make the Frames

Measure the openings and assemble frames made of straight, warp-free 1 by 3s to fit. Attach the pieces with biscuit joints or dowels, or simply use L-shaped brackets and ¾-inch deck screws, as shown. Attach the brackets to both sides.

2 Bend and Clamp the Frames

Lay a frame on a piece of plywood and slide ½-inch-thick plywood strips under the top and bottom of the frame. Slightly bow the center by tightening clamps around the frame and the plywood at the midpoint of the two sides.

3 Attach the Screening

Cut a piece of screening slightly wider and longer than the frame and lay the fabric across the frame. (You may have to remove the clamps temporarily during this stage.) Adjust the mesh so it's at right angles to the frame and staple it across the center of the frame's top edge with rust-proof staples spaced every 2 inches, working from the middle outward. Repeat along the bottom edge. Release the clamps to straighten out the frame and pull the screening taut. Staple the screening to the sides, again working from the middle outward. Trim off the excess screening and attach screen molding to cover up the staples.

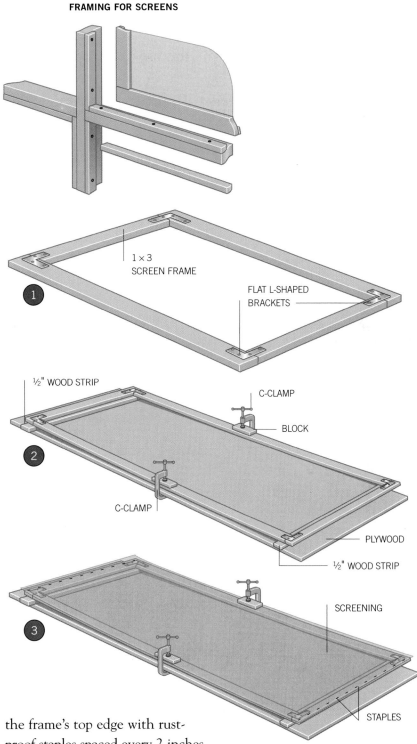

FRAMING FOR SCREENS

1 × 3 SCREEN FRAME

FLAT L-SHAPED BRACKETS

1

½" WOOD STRIP

C-CLAMP

BLOCK

C-CLAMP

2

PLYWOOD

½" WOOD STRIP

SCREENING

3

STAPLES

choosing patio furniture

Wrought iron offers a classic look that can be both formal and whimsical, making it a long-time patio favorite. To ward off rust, you will likely need to touch up chipped paint every one to two years.

Wicker and rattan furniture varies greatly in quality and price. Inexpensive wicker will not last long outdoors, but high-end products can be quite long lived. However, even the best natural wicker should be stored indoors during winter. Plastic "wicker" furniture will never rot, but may look unpleasantly fake and can be prone to warping or sagging.

Resin or plastic furniture, by far the least expensive choice, has come a long way. Even very low-cost chairs and tables are available in a wide array of styles and colors. Resin stays cool in

WROUGHT IRON SEATING SUITE

You can instantly enhance the look of your outdoor room by purchasing classy patio chairs and tables. Choose high-quality furniture that lasts well under conditions in your area, so it will still look great and provide comfort 10 years from now. Pieces that spend a lifetime outdoors need to be exceptionally durable.

RESIN CHAIR

WICKER CHAISE

the sun and requires little maintenance, and chairs often nest for convenient storage. However, long exposure to intense sun can cause the color of plastic furniture, particularly inexpensive pieces, to fade. Store plastic furniture in the shade or keep it covered when not in use.

Aluminum patio furniture is rustproof and strong enough to withstand years of harsh weather. A wide selection of finishes makes aluminum extremely versatile. A "powder" finish is more durable than one that is anodized or simply painted on. Hand-forged wrought-aluminum frames and vinyl strap seating create furniture that is as comfortable as it is durable.

Wood furniture has a timeless appeal. It can last for decades if it is made from a rot-resistant species such as teak, ironwood, or oak. Still, most wood furniture needs a fresh coat of finish every year or so and should be stored indoors during winter.

Make almost any type of chair more comfortable and colorful by adding a padded seat cushion. New synthetic fabrics have the feel of cloth rather than plastic, yet are weather resistant. However, it's a good idea to store cushions in a bin when they are not in use, especially if they would otherwise be exposed to intense sunlight.

Above: *Made of high-quality marine-grade resin, this dining set is comfortable, extremely durable, and almost totally maintenance-free. Resin furniture comes in a variety of styles and colors, and is the least expensive outdoor furniture option, making it a popular choice for patios.*
Right: *Foam-filled cushions make outdoor furniture feel like indoor furniture, yet they can withstand the elements.*

Left: *This furniture uses three different materials for a great combination of sturdiness, classic good looks, and comfort: teak wood for the tabletop and chair arms; aluminum for the chair and table frames; and vinyl mesh for the sling-style seat bottoms and backs.*

51

building furniture

Unless you're a woodworking enthusiast, you probably do not have the skills and tools needed to build chairs or formal pieces of furniture. However, you may want to augment your store-bought furnishings with a simple home-made bench or table. The next six pages give instructions for three such projects that can be built in a day with basic tools.

STORAGE BENCH

This handsome bench can store a couple of hoses, some bags of charcoal, or several pots or garden tools. And it does the job without looking boxy.

The only lumber you'll need is 1-by-6 boards. A tropical hardwood or "ironwood," such as ipé or pau lopé, is ideal. Oak, birch, and teak also work well, but redwood, cedar, and pine are not strong enough.

The key parts of the bench are the front and back legs, which have mitered corner joints and rounded bottoms. The back legs are longer and are tapered in front to form a comfortably angled backrest. The seat is attached to a continuous hinge and is held open with a hook and eye.

For all joints, drill pilot holes, apply glue, then drive screws.

MATERIALS LIST

- Seven 8'-long 1 × 6s for all wood components
- Exterior wood glue or polyurethane glue
- 2" trimhead screws
- 1¼" deck screws
- 48" continuous hinge
- ¼" galvanized wire mesh
- ¾" trusshead screws
- 3½" hook and eye
- Wood sealer, stain, or paint

1 Make the Legs

Set the blade of a table saw or a circular saw to a 45-degree angle and rip (cut lengthwise) in half one 1 by 6. From each half, cut two 16-inch and two 32-inch lengths. Draw identical arcs at the base of each leg—a quart-sized paint can makes a good template—so that each arc bottom ends at the miter joint. Cut the arcs with a jigsaw.

On what will be the side pieces—the backrest—of each back leg, draw the tapered front edge as shown. Make sure the left and right legs mirror each other, then make the tapered cuts. To assemble the legs, apply glue and clamp the pieces together. Then drill pilot holes and drive trim-head screws at about 5-inch intervals.

2 Attach Boards to the Legs

Cut four 1 by 6s at 44 inches (A boards). Attach the boards to the inside of the front and back legs as shown, spaced ½ inch apart. Drive two deck screws into each joint. If you want to run a hose into the bench, drill a 1½-inch hole in the lower rear.

3 Assemble the Lower Bench

Cut four 1 by 6s at 1¾ inches (B boards) and cut six 1 by 6s at 46 inches (five C boards plus D and E boards). Rip one 46-inch length to 2½ inches wide (D board) and three ¾-inch-wide lengths (E boards; one will be

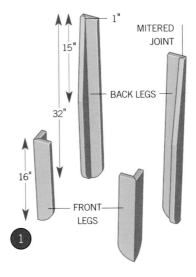

1

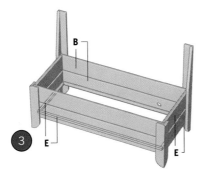

2

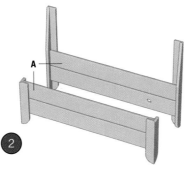

3

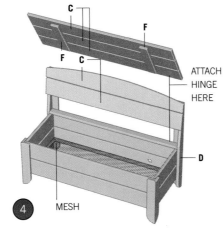

4

cut into two pieces for four total E boards). From the scrap pieces, cut two F boards, which are 2½ inches by 14½ inches.

Attach the B boards with deck screws to join the front and back assemblies. Along the lower inside edges of the A and B boards, use deck screws to attach the E boards that have been cut to fit; they'll support the wire mesh.

4 Add the Seat, Back, and Mesh

Cut the D board to fit between the rear legs and attach it with glue and trimhead screws. Use a hacksaw to cut the continuous hinge to the same length. Use a pencil-and-string compass to sketch an arc with a 7-foot radius on a C board; the arc should start and end 2½ inches above the board's bottom corners. Cut with a jigsaw; this is the top back piece. Using trimhead screws, attach one regular C board and the curved C board to make the backrest.

To assemble the bench seat, place the remaining C boards on a flat surface, spaced evenly, and attach the F boards with deck screws. Center and attach the hinge to the seat's inside back edge, then attach the assembly to the front edge of D.

Cut the wire mesh to fit and attach it to the top of the E boards with trusshead screws. Attach the hook and eye and apply the finish of your choice.

CLASSIC BENCH

The charm of old-fashioned joinery is on display in this simple bench. The mortise-and-tenon joint uses a "tusk"—a small wedge—to both reinforce the joint and add a homey touch. The bench pictured is made of cedar, but you may choose redwood, ironwood, or teak. If 1 by 3s are not available in your choice of wood, buy 1 by 4s and rip-cut the stretcher pieces.

This project calls for some basic woodworking skills. (For a simpler project, see pages 56–57.) A table saw and a drill press make this project easier to accomplish, but you can achieve professional-looking results by carefully using a circular saw and standard drill. To ensure clean and accurate cuts, check that the blades of your jigsaw and circular saw are perfectly square to the base plate. To join the two pieces of each leg, either use a biscuit joiner (which is an inexpensive tool) or drill matching holes and join the pieces with dowels. You will also need to cut tenons on the ends of the stretchers.

MATERIALS LIST

- 1 × 6s for legs and seat pieces
- 1 × 3s for stretchers, tusks, and cleats
- 1¼" deck screws
- Exterior wood glue or polyurethane glue
- Stain and finish, or primer and paint

TOP VIEW

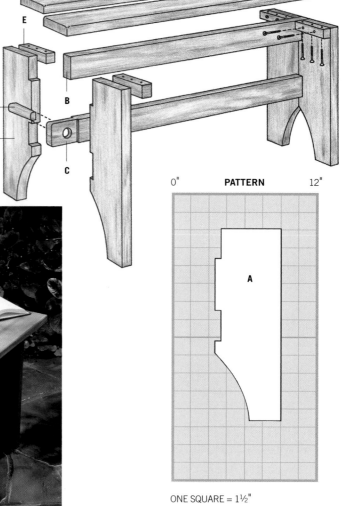

PATTERN
0"   12"

A

ONE SQUARE = 1½"

1 Cut the Leg Pieces

Each leg has two pieces (A). Cut four pieces of 1 by 6 at 16 inches and use the pattern shown (see facing page, bottom) as a guide to mark the pieces for cutting. Cut the notches using a table saw or clamp the pieces together and use a circular saw (see page 45). Then cut the curves with a jigsaw. Sand the edges smooth.

2 Assemble the Legs

To firmly join the two pieces of each leg, use a biscuit joiner to cut slots in the mating edges. Or, drill holes for dowels. Then apply glue and dowels or biscuits, and clamp the pieces together.

3 Make and Install the Stretchers

Cut one 1 by 3 at 30 inches (B, the top stretcher) and one at 34 inches (C, the bottom stretcher). Use a handsaw and a chisel to cut a 1-inch-long, $^{3}/_{4}$-inch-wide tenon on both ends of the top stretcher and a $3^{3}/_{4}$-inch-long, $^{3}/_{4}$-inch-wide tenon on both ends of the bottom stretcher. Sand or file a $^{1}/_{4}$-inch chamfer on the ends of the long tenons.

Drill a 1-inch hole in either end of the bottom stretcher, $1^{3}/_{4}$ inches in from each end, to accept the tusks. Cut two tusks (D) 4 inches long and 1 inch wide and file or plane a gentle taper on one side.

4 Assemble the Bench

Glue the stretchers into the mortises in the legs and drive a tusk through the holes in the bottom stretcher. Cut four cleats (E) $1^{1}/_{4}$ inches by 5 inches and attach them to either side of the top stretcher by drilling pilot holes and driving deck screws. Cut three seat pieces at $4^{1}/_{2}$ inches by $37^{1}/_{2}$ inches (F). Center the pieces over the legs with $^{1}/_{4}$-inch spaces between the pieces. Drill pilot holes and drive deck screws to attach the seat pieces to the cleats. Sand the bench and apply the finish of your choice.

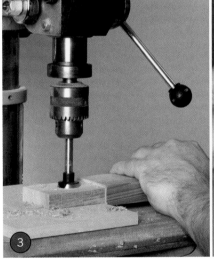

END TABLE

This attractive patio table is built with no fancy joints; if you can saw a board and drive a screw, you can build it. The size and shape of the ends can be modified to suit your needs or to complement other furnishings. For instance, you might choose to leave the ends square to form a rectangular top or cut a gentle curve after the top has been installed.

For all joints, drill pilot holes, apply glue, and drive screws.

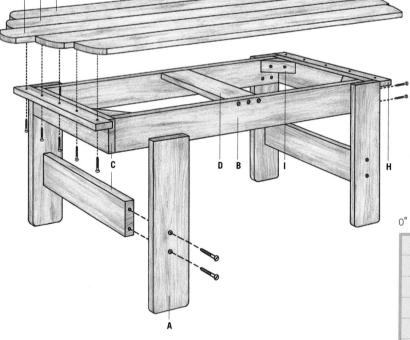

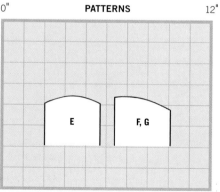

PATTERNS

0"   12"

E

F, G

ONE SQUARE = 1½"

1 Assemble the Legs and Aprons

For the legs (A), cut four 1 by 4s at 16 inches and round the corners with a file or sanding block. Cut two aprons (B) at 30 inches, four stretchers (C) at 17 inches, and one brace (D) at 15½ inches. Using 2-inch screws, build a rectangle composed of the aprons and two stretchers; attach the brace in the middle of the frame. Attach the legs as shown, so they run past the stretchers by ¾ inch. Clamp the legs and check for square before drilling pilot holes and driving 1¼-inch screws.

2 Attach the Lower Stretchers

Flip the table upright. Make a pair of 4½-inch spacer blocks to position the lower stretchers, as shown. Center the stretcher on the legs, clamp, and recheck the position before drilling pilot holes and driving 2-inch screws.

3 Assemble the Seat Slats

Cut the five seat slats (E, F, and G) so that they overhang the frame by at least 2 inches at either end. To follow the design pictured, use the patterns. Lay the seat slats face down on a flat surface and insert ¼-inch spacers between them. Center the frame upside down on the slats from end to end and from side to side. Cut two cleats (H) at 1¾ inches by 18½ inches. Position the cleats on the ends so that they snug up against the frame and attach them to the slats with 1¼-inch screws.

4 Attach Corner Blocks and Finish

Pick the frame off the seat slats and flip it right side up. Cut four corner blocks (I) out of 2 by 4. Drive two 1⅝-inch screws to attach a block to each corner so that the blocks are flush with the top of the frame. Flip the frame over and place it onto the seat slats. Drive a screw through each corner block and into a seat slat. Sand the entire project and apply the finish of your choice.

MATERIALS LIST

- Concrete for posts
- Gravel
- Pressure-treated 2 × 4s for the framing and ledger
- 4 × 4 pressure-treated posts
- ¾" exterior or pressure-treated plywood
- Aluminum "drip cap" flashing, 6" wide
- 3" deck screws
- 1" roofing nails
- 8d galvanized nails
- 1 × 2 for shelf edging
- Roofing felt and shingles
- Plywood siding
- 1 × 4 for trim

storage shelter

This handsome recycle center houses trash cans and recycling bins, eliminating eyesores and keeping things dry. You can also use the shelter to store garden supplies. It's a fairly easy project that a fairly handy person with a basic set of carpentry tools can build in a day or two.

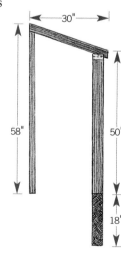

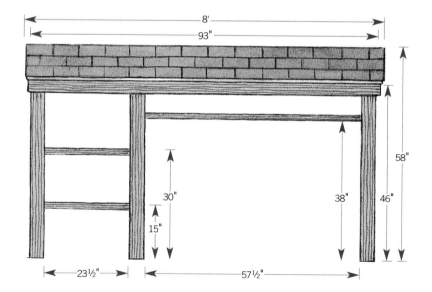

1 Set the Posts and Frame
Cut the 2-by-4 ledger at 90 inches. Hold the ledger level against the house, 58 inches above the ground, and drive deck screws to fasten it snugly.

Cut three 2-by-4 vertical supports to fit against the wall under the ledger. Using deck screws, attach two of the vertical supports under either end of the ledger, allowing 1½ inches to extend beyond the

ledger at each end; these extensions will support the outer two rafters. Fasten a third support to the house so that there is 23½ inches of space between it and the left vertical support.

Dig three 18-inch-deep post holes in line with the vertical boards on the house wall and 22¼ inches in front of the boards. Hold the posts in place with temporary bracing; check that they are square and plumb. Mix the concrete and fill the holes. Let the concrete cure for a day or so. (Alternatively, wait until the structure is completed before pouring the concrete.) Cut off the top of the center post 46 inches above ground level. Cut the tops off the other two posts so that they are level with the center post.

To make a top plate, cut two 2 by 4s to 93 inches. Fasten them together across the top of the posts to support the rafters. Cut the rafters from 2 by 4s. To make

one of the side rafters, hold a 2 by 4 in place against the house, resting on the ledger and the top plate. Use a level to mark for plumb cuts at either end; the rafter should overhang the top plate by 2 inches. Hold the cut piece in place and mark for the "bird's-mouth" notches where the rafter fits over the top plate. Use this first rafter as a template for the others; make the two middle rafters 1½ inches shorter than the end rafters. Space the rafters evenly and attach them with angle-driven nails or screws at both ends.

Cut seven 2-by-4 shelf supports to fit between the posts and the vertical supports. Position them at the desired heights for the shelves, check for level, and attach with nails or screws.

2 Install the Shelves and Roof

Cut plywood shelves to fit over the shelf supports and attach them with nails. For the roof, cut

plywood to fit over the rafters so that it overhangs by an inch or so on both sides. Attach with nails.

3 Add the Roofing, the Sides, and the Floor

Use tin snips to cut drip cap flashing to fit on the outer three edges of the roof and attach with 1-inch roofing nails. Staple roofing paper to the plywood and finish the roof with shingles or other roofing to match the house roof.

Add the plywood siding to both sides of the structure (here, ⅜-inch redwood siding and 2½-inch battens were used). To conceal the rafters and trim the top and bottom edges on each end, install 1 by 4s to fit. Finish the front edge of each shelf with 1 by 2s cut to fit between the posts; first glue them, then drive screws or nails.

Add a patio floor if desired. Sand the wood pieces, apply a coat of primer, and paint.

container gardening

Left: *Openings in the patio can be filled with soil and plants, or with potted plants.* **Below:** *These planters are made of the same concrete as the patio below them. Although plain gray concrete can have an unpleasantly industrial look, adding just a touch of texture and color has a stunning effect.* **Bottom:** *These potted plants are arranged with the shortest in front and the tallest in back, to show them off to full advantage and create the feel of a dense jungle.*

A container garden is wonderfully versatile. You can choose the containers, the plants that go in them, and where the containers will be placed. You can showcase the plants that are in full bloom and have glorious foliage and move to the back those that are at an awkward stage of growth.

In a cold climate, you'll be pleasantly surprised if you set your indoor plants out on the patio for the summer. Many of these plants will thrive in ways they never could indoors, and will not suffer ill effects when moved back inside for the winter.

Just about any container—olive oil can, galvanized tub, watering can, even an old work boot—can serve as a planter. Inexpensive clay pots look great when filled with foliage; either enjoy the inevitable whitish water stains, or occasionally brush them away with linseed oil. Terra-cotta and ceramic glazed pots add texture and color. Clay sewer pipes provide a vertical dimension.

Containers are not just for flowers. A few pots or a large planter can hold basil, rosemary, thyme, and other herbs to enliven your cooking. Tomatoes, especially "patio" varieties, are easy to cultivate and harvest when planted in large containers. String beans, cucumbers, peppers, squashes, leeks, green onions, and peas are also fine candidates for container gardening. Strawberries actually thrive best in containers.

BUILDING A WOOD PLANTER

A planter is basically a box made of rot-resistant material with drainage holes in the bottom. The outside of the planter can be dressed up any way you want.

There are two basic types of wood planters: those filled with soil and those used to house flowerpots. A soil-filled planter must be extremely resistant to rot. To make yours highly resistant, build the planter, then hire a sheet-metal shop (or gutter-supply company) to make a galvanized box that fits inside the planter. The bottom of a planter for flowerpots must be made of a very rot-resistant material, such as pressure-treated lumber, but the sides can be made of cedar or redwood.

Both types of planter must have ample drainage at the bottom. Either install bottom slats spaced about ¼ inch apart or drill a grid of ⅜-inch holes. If the planter will be filled with soil, place a layer of gravel at least 3 inches deep in the bottom before you add the soil.

All the visible boards in this planter are made of inexpensive 1-by cedar fencing, which is rough on both sides. For a cleaner look, use regular smooth-sided 1-bys or ⁵⁄₄ decking. Stainless-steel screws add a subtle touch of class without much additional expense, but you may choose to use deck screws instead.

MATERIALS LIST

- 1× cedar fencing for the sides and trim
- Pressure-treated 1 × 2 for cleats at bottom
- Pressure-treated ⁵⁄₄ × 6 decking for the floor pieces
- Exterior wood glue or polyurethane glue
- 1¼" deck screws
- 2" stainless-steel screws
- Wood stain or sealer

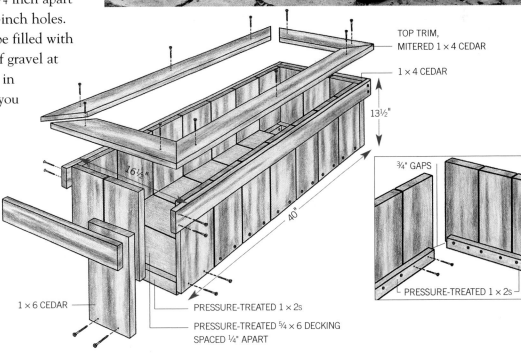

TOP TRIM, MITERED 1 × 4 CEDAR

1 × 4 CEDAR

13½"

16½"

40"

¾" GAPS

PRESSURE-TREATED 1 × 2s

1 × 6 CEDAR

PRESSURE-TREATED 1 × 2s

PRESSURE-TREATED ⁵⁄₄ × 6 DECKING SPACED ¼" APART

2 Construct the Sides

For each side, place the vertical pieces against each other with the finished sides down. Use a framing square to make sure they are aligned to form a rectangle. Cut a 1-by-2 cleat 3 inches shorter than the length of the assembled vertical pieces. Position the 1 by 2 so it hangs below the bottom of the vertical pieces by about ¼ inch, keeping the vertical pieces from resting on the patio. Leave a ¾-inch gap at either end of the 1 by 2. Apply glue, drill pilot holes, and drive two 1¼-inch deck screws through the 1 by 2 and into the vertical pieces.

3 Assemble the Sides and Floor

Hold two sides together with the shorter side covering the edge of the longer side. Using a framing square to see that the two pieces are at right angles, hold the pieces flush and drill pilot holes. Apply glue and drive 2-inch screws.

After all four sides are assembled, cut pieces of pressure-treated floor pieces to fit and set them on top of the 1-by-2 cleats. If the planter will hold flowerpots, space the floor pieces as much as 2 inches apart; if you will fill the planter with soil, leave only ¼-inch spaces. Check the planter for square, then drill pilot holes and drive 2-inch screws to attach the floor pieces to the 1-by-2 cleats. From the outside of the planter, drive 2-inch screws through the vertical pieces and into the floor pieces.

1 Cut and Sand the Pieces

Cut the 1 by 6 vertical pieces at 13½ inches. The planter shown has seven pieces on the sides and three on the ends, but you can change the shape and size by using more or fewer pieces. Use a sanding block to round off the edges of the pieces, both to minimize splinters and to visually emphasize the planter's vertical lines.

4 Trim the Top

Rip-cut trim pieces 3 inches wide. Measure and cut pieces to fit around the top of the planter. Attach them with 2-inch screws at the corners and then drive 1¼-inch screws from the inside of the vertical pieces. Miter-cut the top trim, as shown, or straight-cut the pieces for a more rustic look. Attach the top trim using 2-inch screws.

installing a micro-sprinkler system

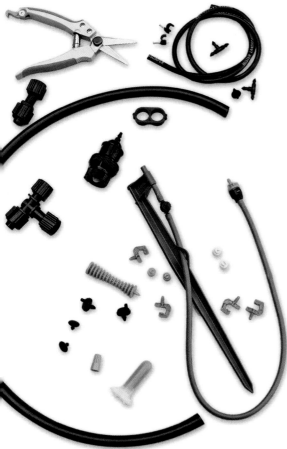

With modest cost and only a few hours of labor, you can install a system that automatically waters your containers and flower beds.

Microirrigation (once called drip irrigation) uses easy-to-install parts to deliver just the right amount of water to small plantings. Unlike installing a lawn sprinkler system, there is no need to measure your home's water pressure, make complicated calculations, dig trenches for pipes, or plan for various zones. Instead, you install a simple control valve, run flexible hoses, make easy poke-in connections, and press sprinklers or drip emitters into the soil.

PLANNING ROUTES AND CHOOSING PARTS

Run the water from a convenient water source, such as an outdoor faucet, to the plants. There is no need to draw up a detailed plan for your system. Read pages 64 and 65, then take measurements around your patio to get a general idea of how much flexible hose and tubing and which sprinklers and emitters you will need.

At a home center or hardware store, you will likely find both individual parts as well as microsprinkler kits that contain nearly all the parts you need. Kits are inexpensive, so it's sensible to buy one even if it has some parts you will not need. If you later find that you need more sprinkler heads or stakes of a certain type, simply go back to the store and buy some more.

While all the little parts that make up a microsprinkler system may make the job look complicated, you'll soon find that it's really straightforward. In addition to ½-inch hose and ¼-inch tubing, you'll need a controller, a punch tool, fittings, stakes, and emitters or spray heads. Some spray heads are easily adjusted to squirt water in a full circle, half circle, quarter circle, and so on. Larger sprinkler heads may come already attached to a stake. To cut the lines, you need only garden shears (dead-headers), utility scissors, or a knife.

Microspray

Drip head

Bow-tie spray

Tee fitting

Multioutlet fitting

Fittings for ½-inch hose are usually compression type, meaning that you slip the hose in and tighten a nut. Fittings for ¼-inch tubing are even simpler: just push the tubing onto the barb and you're done. If you want to have three or more ¼-inch lines branch off from a single point, use a multioutlet fitting.

HOOK UP TO THE WATER SUPPLY

Usually, it's best to run ½-inch hose to the general location of the plants and then branch off with ¼-inch lines that run to individual containers. (Running ¼-inch tubing for more than 15 feet or so will inhibit water pressure.) However, if you have only a short distance to travel and fewer than eight plants to water, you may choose to run only ¼-inch tubing. The smaller tubing has the advantage of being less visible.

It is possible to hook up directly to a cold-water supply

pipe in your home, but connecting to a hose faucet is easier. The simplest arrangement is to screw a wye valve onto the faucet and then screw a small control valve to one leg of the wye; you can hook a garden hose to the other side of the wye. The control valve is battery operated and allows you to set the system to turn on and off at the same time or times every day. It contains a backflow-prevention device to protect your home water from contamination as well as a screen to keep debris in the water from clogging sprinkler heads.

Simple control valve

Separate control valves

If you want to water at different times on different days, or if you have two or more areas that you want to water separately, install separate control valves as shown. You will need to run thin wires to a location inside the house and hook them to a programmable timer.

Programmable timer

RUN ½-INCH HOSE

The ½-inch flexible hose (sometimes called drip hose) used in microirrigation systems is easily kinked, so uncoil it carefully and make only gradual turns. If you do accidentally kink the line, cut it on either side of the kink and install a coupling; otherwise, water flow will be greatly impeded.

Attach the hose to the control valve and tighten the nut. You can run the line on top of the ground and cover it with mulch or run it through a shallow trench. If the hose is stepped on it will be damaged, so protect it with a board or run in it a 4-inch-deep trench wherever there is foot traffic.

Figure-eight closure

Goof plug

Threading ¼-inch tubing

Route the hose so that it comes within 6 feet or so of the containers. Cut the end and install a figure-eight closure at the end of the line.

BRANCH OFF WITH ¼-INCH LINES

To attach ¼-inch tubing, poke a hole in the hose using a punch tool. Then insert a barbed fitting and slip the tubing onto the fitting. Tubing is easier to work with than hose because it does not kink easily. However, it is easily compressed, so protect it from getting squished by foot traffic.

Punch tool

Barbed fitting

If you poke a hole in the wrong place or later decide to eliminate a line, insert a goof plug to seal the hole.

Tubing can be run in several different ways. You can run it on top of the soil and cover with mulch, thread it between pavers, or just sneak it behind flowerpots. If you need to run tubing along wood members of a railing or an overhead, fasten it with tubing staples every 16 inches or so.

SPRINKLERS AND EMITTERS

To deliver the right amount of water to the right place, you may need to experiment a bit. Containers should be filled with water, not just have water sprayed at only one portion of the soil. For small and medium pots, a single sprayer usually does the job. For a large pot, use a tee, run tubing to either side, and install two sprinklers.

In most cases, you will run tubing to a stake, screw a sprinkler head onto the stake, and then poke the stake into the soil. Turn the water on to test. You will likely need to adjust the location of the stake or change the sprinkler head to get the watering pattern you want. If a

plant needs only a small amount of water, install a drip emitter rather than a sprinkler head.

To water a hanging plant, string the hose into the pot and poke an emitter directly into the tubing.

Two sprinklers with a tee

Emitter for hanging plant

crevice plants

Low-growing crevice plants ornament the space between flagstones on this patio. Accents of lavender and ivy add story-book charm.

Some nurseries have a special section, perhaps called "steppables," for those low-growing plants that can survive being walked on and that can be planted in small cracks. Crevice plants are often an integral part of a patio, adding color and texture and softening the appearance of stone or brick.

Choose plants that will survive in your area and that are compatible with the type of soil and amount of water they will receive. If the patio often develops puddles or the soil around it is dense, mosses are a good choice; if the soil is well drained and sandy and the area is often

dry, thyme and other desert plants will do well.

Remove all weeds before planting. Once established, many weeds (such as common grass) have roots that reach deep. If you cannot pull up a weed's roots, spray it with a weed killer and wait a couple of weeks before planting.

In general, larger plants survive well only in low-traffic areas; plants with small leaves are less crushable. Succulents look fragile, but some types are surprisingly hardy. Herbs like thyme and marjoram release a pleasant aroma when stepped on.

Buy plants rather than seeds; young shoots are very fragile. Break the plants into small pieces and dig a hole deep enough so that the roots don't have to be balled up when you plant. Set the plants several inches apart, then fill in with soil or sand.

To propagate moss, make a slurry: find and scrape up local moss growing in a spot similar to where you will plant. In a bucket, mix a solution of one part moss (which will come attached to a fair amount of soil) with one part buttermilk and stir until fairly smooth. Use a spoon or paintbrush to slather on the mixture where you want it to grow.

Left: Geranium, blue sedge, heliotrope, blue and white alyssum. *Below:* Blue star creeper.

Above: Moss pink, snow-in-summer, and silver lace. *Right:* Blue thyme and blue star creeper.

Above: Meadow foam.

water features

Just about any patio area can benefit from the sound of trickling water, the glint of sunlight on the water's surface, and the exotic plants that live in water. If you have the yard space, consider a pond like the one shown on pages 70–71.

FOUNTAIN IN A POT

A container fountain will fit anywhere and can be set on a patio or a bench. All you need is a submersible pump, access to an electrical outlet, a container, and the rocks and plants of your choice. The fountain portion can be entirely submersed, so that water bubbles up to the surface, or you can buy a fountain-head attachment that causes water to spray or cascade.

This project features a variation on a traditional Japanese design called the shishi-odoshi, or "deer scarer." Since bamboo is mostly hollow, you can easily make a bamboo pipe and spout yourself, though you may need to do a little drilling to completely hollow out the stalk. Tie the pieces together using decorative twine or copper wire, which will eventually turn a pleasant green. Or, buy a pre-assembled bamboo fountain at a nursery or garden supply source.

The pot used in this project was sealed and glazed. If the one you choose is not watertight, apply a coat of acrylic masonry sealer or a sealer made especially for water gardens. If your container has a hole in the bottom, fill it with a plug and coat it with a layer of two-part epoxy glue (the type typically used to repair plates and cups). Once dry, the glue will provide a firm seal.

1 Attach the Pump

Rinse out the container and wash the rocks. Run the extension cord to an outdoor GFCI-protected electrical receptacle but do not plug it in. Attach a piece of clear vinyl tubing to the pump's outlet. Place the pump on its side in the bottom of the container with a few rocks around it to hold it in place.

MATERIALS LIST

- Watertight container
- Small submersible pump
- Extension cord
- Clear vinyl tubing (usually supplied with the pump)
- River rocks
- Slabs of slate and flagstone
- Bamboo spout
- Submersible plant dish
- Plant that grows in water

2 Add the Plant and Rocks

Place the water plant, such as this miniature umbrella plant, in the submersible dish. If the dish will be visible, choose one that complements the color of the stones. Place the plant dish on the bottom of the container and snake the pump's power cord behind it. Add more base rocks.

3 Set Up the Fountain

Thread the tubing up through the bamboo and place the bamboo on the edge of the container. Then pull the rest of the tubing through, cut off any excess, and attach the spout. Position the spout to point toward the rocks you want to hit with water.

4 Add the Top Rocks and Test the Fountain

Add and arrange the remaining rocks. Fill the container with water—the water level need not be higher than the pump. Plug in the pump and check that the water moves smoothly through the tubing. When the pump makes a humming sound, more water is needed.

garden pools

Apond with bubbling water lends a soothing bit of enchantment to an outdoor space. If you want a large pond or would like to custom-design the shape, you'll need to install a flexible liner, which is a fairly complex project; consult a book such as Sunset's *Garden Pools, Fountains & Waterfalls*. Installing a preformed rigid pond liner such as the one shown here is a much simpler procedure.

Position the pond where it will receive enough light to support the water plants you have chosen. Either place the pond well away from trees or expect to regularly skim away fallen leaves.

Buy a fountain that is the right size for the pool. You can choose among fountain spray heads that bubble or spray at various heights. Some fountain heads even produce sprays in a bell or tulip shape. The fountain rests in the bottom of the pool; it is a good idea to anchor it with two or three flat rocks. Most fountains plug into a standard GFCI-protected electrical receptacle. If your site is sunny, you can install a solar-powered fountain, which does not need to be plugged in.

1 Mark the Outline

In a flat, open area, remove sod and any plants. Set the pond liner, right side up, in place. Mark its outline by scratching a line in the soil. You will likely need to draw two outlines, one for the shallower shelves and one for the deeper portion. Remove the liner and emphasize the outline by pouring flour or sand on it.

2 Dig and Place the Liner

Dig a hole 2 inches wider and 2 inches deeper than the liner. Remove any roots and stones as you work. Set the liner in the hole (it should be 2 inches deeper than grade) and mark the areas where you need to dig deeper. Once you have finished digging, add 2 inches of sand and set the liner in the hole. Check that the liner is level in both directions. If it is more than ½ inch out of level, pick up the liner and adjust the sand as needed.

3 Fill and Backfill

Start filling the liner with a slow trickle of water. At the same time, begin backfilling by placing a 4-inch layer of sand around the outside of the liner. Tamp down the sand around the liner with a short scrap of wood. Add and tamp more layers of sand to fill the space around the liner and support it at all points.

4 Add Decorative Edging

Edge the pond with stones to hide the liner's rim. Make sure most of each stone's weight rests on soil, not on the liner. Set the fountain in the pool, anchor it with stones, and plug it in. Adjust its position to suit your taste. Cover the cord with mulch or run it through a shallow trench, then add the plants of your choice.

patio lighting

Good lighting makes a walkway easy to navigate after dark, provides safety and security, and creates a welcoming ambiance. Flexibility is the key. Bright standard-voltage lights, such as an under-eave porch light or a post light, add strong illumination to repel intruders or allow you to walk without tripping when carrying in the groceries. However, they are too glaring for entertaining. Low-voltage lights are mellower, and bright enough for most evening activities. For most patios, a combination of the two types of lighting is ideal. If you already have strong standard-voltage lighting, consider installing dimmer switches so that you can soften the effect when you want.

LANTERN-TYPE LIGHT

LIGHTS TO CHOOSE

A good selection of low-voltage lights is available at most home centers. Don't stop looking there, however; pick up a catalog or two from lighting manufacturers or type "low-voltage lighting" into a search engine. You'll find a stunning array of lights from which to choose; the variety of prices is nearly as stunning.

PATH LIGHT

FLOODLIGHT

Path lights usually have shades that produce a wide, downward spread of light. Lantern-type lights both illuminate paths and provide general lighting. Spotlights or floodlights can be swiveled to point at a feature or an area of the yard. "Brick lights" are shaped to resemble a patio paver and are actually installed in the soil, where they point diffused light upward. Rope lights are strings of tiny, evenly spaced bulbs that can be draped along a railing or hung from a tree like Christmas lights. Deck lights can be fastened to a vertical structure such as an overhead or a trellis.

The least expensive option will likely be a kit that contains 10 or so lights, a programmable transformer, and all the cable and connectors you need. If you want to install a variety of lights or if you don't like the lights that come in kits, you will need to purchase the components separately. When purchasing a transformer, check its specs or consult with a salesperson to be sure that it is strong enough to supply power to all the lights you need.

PORTABLE "ROCK" LIGHTS

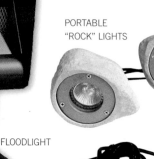

LIGHTING TECHNIQUES

Position lights so that they will provide illumination without shining into people's eyes. Often, this means placing low-voltage lights lower than 2 feet above the ground and standard-voltage lights higher than 7 feet. You can also place lights behind a barrier or use fixtures that provide shielded or diffused light. Most yards benefit from a combination of two or three of these types:

DOWNLIGHTING Use lights that point downward to gently light up a patio or walkway, or to accent trees and shrubs.

Downlighting

SILHOUETTING To emphasize the shape of a tree, shrub, or bed of flowers, try aiming a spotlight or floodlight at a fence or wall from close behind the plant.

SPREAD LIGHTING Use short downward-spreading lights not only to light up a path but to light up shrubbery or flowers. Try different-colored bulbs for decorative effects.

Spread lighting

Silhouetting

SENSORS

Attached to the right switches, landscape and security lights can virtually take care of themselves. Daylight sensors, also called photocells or photovoltaic switches, turn a light on when it gets dark. You can install fixtures with built-in sensors or buy the sensors separately. Some mount to an electrical box or a post and others can be screwed into a light socket.

Many inexpensive porch lights have a motion sensor that turns the light on when it senses motion at night. You can adjust the sensor for sensitivity and light duration and point it toward the area of your choice. Replacing a standard porch light with one of these units is usually a simple procedure.

MOTION SENSOR

DAYLIGHT SENSORS

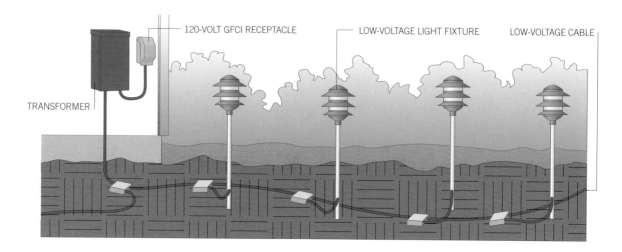

TRANSFORMER   120-VOLT GFCI RECEPTACLE   LOW-VOLTAGE LIGHT FIXTURE   LOW-VOLTAGE CABLE

INSTALLING A LOW-VOLTAGE LIGHT SYSTEM

Installing low-voltage lights calls for no special electrician skills. You simply plug the system into a GFCI receptacle. Since the wires carry only 12 volts of power, you do not need to get an electrical permit. You also don't need to dig trenches for the wires; in most cases you can just cover them with a thin layer of soil or mulch. However, you will need to plan the paths carefully so the wires will not get tangled or trampled.

If you have no outdoor receptacle, you may be able to drill a hole in your house's siding, run the wires through, and plug them into an indoor receptacle. If you need a new receptacle, consult with an electrician.

1 Mount the Transformer

Near a GFCI receptacle and in a spot where it is not likely to get bumped, mount the transformer by driving screws into the house's siding or a fence.

2 Run the Wire

Lay the lights on the ground, positioned where you want them. Starting at the transformer (leave yourself a couple of extra feet just in case), run the wires past the lights. Wherever people are likely to walk, dig a trench for the wires at least 6 inches deep; elsewhere, dig a shallower trench or simply cover the wires with mulch.

3 Make the Connections

Each light has a length of wire that connects to the main wire. Join the wires using the connectors provided. Some connections simply snap together while others are screwed together. While the connectors are easy to attach, you still need to work carefully to make sure the connections are tight and secure.

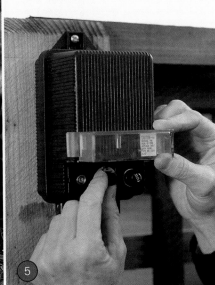

4 Install the Lights and Cover the Wires

If your soil is soft, you can probably just poke each of the lights on the run into the ground with your hands. If you have hard soil, you may first need to slice the ground with a garden trowel or a shovel and then poke the light into the slice. When all the lights are set, cover the wires with mulch or soil. Where people will walk, bury the wires in a trench at least 4 inches deep.

5 Program the Transformer

Run the main wire to the transformer, anchoring it with staples if needed to keep it from becoming a tripping hazard. Cut the wire to length, separate the strands, strip ¾ inch of insulation from the ends, and attach the bare ends to the transformer's terminals. Follow the manufacturer's instructions to program the lights to turn on and off at certain times, or simply have them come on when it gets dark.

6 Plug in the Transformer

An in-use cover, as shown, protects the receptacle and the plug from rain while the lights are plugged in. Plug the transformer in. Check the lights during the night and adjust the transformer if needed.

SOLAR LIGHTS

Here's the final word in ease of installation: just poke a solar light into the ground and you're done; no wires are needed. As long as the solar panel receives at least four hours of sunlight per day, the light will provide steady—though certainly not overly bright—illumination at night. It may take a few days for the battery to fully energize.

sprucing up concrete

An old concrete slab is probably functional, but may be less than pleasing to the eye. If the concrete is in sound condition, you have a number of options for making it more attractive. You can:

- Clean it
- Apply a skim coat or top coat (see page 77)
- Color it by applying acid stain, a polymer coating, or paint (pages 78–81)
- Pave over it with flagstone, tile, pebble mosaics, or brick (pages 168–79)

If the slab is not sound, you probably need to demolish it and start again. If you like, you can reuse the concrete chunks to make a flagstonelike patio surface (see pages 130–31). But before you decide to demolish your patio, inspect it carefully.

INSPECTING THE SLAB

A close surface examination will usually tell you whether damage to your patio is structural or only cosmetic.

- Occasional cracks are cosmetic as long as both sides of the crack are the same height. To repair a crack, see instructions at right.
- Medium to large cracks indicate a more serious problem, especially if one side of a crack is higher than the other. Such cracks will likely grow larger in time. If any part of the slab feels wobbly, then the slab should be replaced.
- A web of hairline cracks is called "crazing." Bubblelike deterioration and/or flaking of the surface is called "spalling" or "scaling." Small holes scattered throughout a concrete surface are called "popouts." All three problems are probably caused by poor finishing when a slab is installed. And while all three affect only the surface, if left untreated they can cause the top of the slab to crumble, especially in areas with cold winters. Resurfacing (see page 77) is the solution. Crazing or spalling in only one area will require repair rather than resurfacing.

MINOR CONCRETE REPAIRS

To fill a crack, use patching cement that is vinyl or latex reinforced. Use a hammer and a cold chisel to "key" the crack—chip it at an angle to make the bottom of the crack wider than the top (above right). Clean out all loose material using a wire brush or a strong spray from a hose. Paint the crack with latex concrete bonding agent. Mix a small batch of patching cement so that it is just barely pourable, then use a trowel to stuff the patch into the crack. Scrape the surface so that the top of the patch is at the same height as the slab (right middle).

If an area of the slab has surface damage, cut lines around the area to a depth of about ½ inch using a circular saw equipped with a masonry blade. Chip out the center, brush on latex concrete bonding agent, and fill the area with concrete patching compound (bottom).

CLEANING AND SEALING CONCRETE

A thorough cleaning can make disgusting-looking concrete at least acceptable. Purchase a degreasing product for cleaning garage floors or buy a commercial concrete cleaner. Scrub and rinse the concrete two or three times.

If stains remain, try washing with a muriatic-acid solution. Acid cleaning often renders the aggregate—the sand and little pebbles in concrete—more visible, a look you may find attractive. (However, acid-cleaned concrete cannot later be acid stained.) Wearing protective clothing and acid-resistant rubber gloves, mix a solution of 5 parts water to 1 part muriatic acid. Always add acid to the water; never add water to the acid. Pour the acid mixture onto the concrete, scrub with a brush, then rinse it off thoroughly. If this mild solution does not do the trick, try scrubbing with a stronger solution—3, 2, or even 1 part water to 1 part acid.

Sealing concrete is simple and effective. Just brush on acrylic concrete sealer or an all-purpose acrylic sealer. The sealer will produce a slightly shiny surface that resists water infiltration.

SKIM COATING

At a home center or masonry supply source, you will find several durable concrete resurfacing products. Though typically applied only ¼ to ½ inch thick, the resulting surface is quite strong.

To apply, clean the old concrete and patch any cracks. Work when the sun is not shining directly on the surface or the resurfacer may dry too quickly. Mix the resurfacer with water to produce a paste that is just pourable. Working quickly, use a magnesium float or a broom-handled squeegee to spread the paste at a uniform thickness. Use a damp brush to finish any edges that are not smooth.

TOP COATING

If a slab is firm but uneven, or if you want to strengthen a slab, apply a top coat that is 1½ to 2 inches thick. Dig a narrow trench around the perimeter of the slab. Cut and place 2 by 4s against the concrete, 1 to 2 inches above the surface of the concrete. Drive stakes every 3 feet and anchor them to the 2 by 4s with screws. Brush or roll a coat of latex concrete bonding agent onto the concrete.

Skim coating

Empty a bag of sand-mix concrete into a wheelbarrow and add a shovel or two of Portland cement. Mix in water to produce a stiff concrete that needs to be shoveled rather than poured. Apply the top coat to the old concrete and follow the instructions on pages 182–86 to screed and finish the surface.

Top coating

acid-staining concrete

Acid-staining concrete produces a look so attractive that many people use it to produce beautiful interior floors and countertops. While interior applications are best left to the pros, with the right materials and careful preparation you can successfully stain an outdoor concrete surface.

By penetrating beneath the surface, acid stain creates a finish that is extremely durable. The acid reacts with the concrete, which is composed of several materials, to yield an appearance that is pleasantly mottled, sometimes with marblelike veins.

A local paint store may carry acid stain products, but you will find a wider range of colors if you type "acid stain concrete" into a search engine. The color charts for these products give only a fair approximation of the color you will end up with.

PREPARING THE SLAB

Acid stain works well as long as the concrete it is applied to is smooth and clean. If the concrete has a broomed finish or if its top layer has worn so that sand and small pebbles are visible, then the stain will not produce vivid color unless you apply an overlay (see top of page 79).

The final color depends partly on the color of the concrete.

Stain applied to light-colored concrete will create bright colors; stain applied to dark-gray concrete will produce a more subtle—though still attractive—effect. If your concrete has been patched, the patches will almost certainly end up as a different color from the rest.

It is very important that you thoroughly clean the concrete before applying the stain. Even if an old concrete surface looks uniform in color, it almost certainly is covered with oils that will inhibit the staining process. Apply commercial concrete cleaner and scrub with a stiff-bristled brush, then rinse and repeat. Be sure to rinse away all soap residue. Do not wash the surface with a muriatic-acid solution; this will expose the sand and pebbles in the concrete.

Examine the surface closely, both when wet and when dry.

Above: Staining a concrete slab with two shades of brown creates a patio that feels like a natural part of the yard. Below: All of these concrete sections were first stained the same color; then a darker stain was applied to the sections in the foreground. This technique ensures that the differently stained areas complement each other.

Any discoloration will probably be heightened rather than masked by the stain you apply.

If the surface is rough, has been patched, or has cracks you would like to hide, you can apply an overlay product, available from some concrete stain supply sources, before applying the stain. The overlay is strong and hard as long as it is mixed with the right amount of water—too much water will weaken it. Mix the overlay according to directions and trowel onto the concrete using a magnesium float or a steel trowel (see pages 185–86). Hold the trowel nearly flat as you smooth the mixture. Unless you have experience finishing concrete, you will end up with subtle ridges and valleys, but these are not out of place on an outdoor surface.

Applying overlay

THE BASIC APPLICATION

Here we show how to stain an area all the same color. Begin with a slab that is completely clean and dry. Use sheets of plywood or plastic to protect any nearby lawn and plants from overspray. Cover any wood edging with vinyl tape (commonly sold as electrician's bundling tape). Wear a long-sleeved shirt and long pants, protective eyewear, and heavy-duty rubber gloves.

If you use a bristle or polyester brush, applying the stain may ruin the bristles, so you'll need to throw the brush away after use. A nylon brush will survive acid staining.

Avoid applying the stain while the sun is shining on the concrete or on a hot, dry day. If the stain dries quickly, you could end up with uneven color when you apply wet stain to a dry edge.

Pour the stain into a pump sprayer. In most cases you will want to use full-strength stain, but you can dilute the stain with water if you desire a light color. Have a helper spray the area while you use a brush to work the stain into the concrete with firm circular motions. A slight bubbling or fizzing will occur. Maintain a wet edge as you work across the slab.

Applying stain

Unless you want brush strokes to show, spray a fine mist of stain over the surface once it has begun to dry.

Allow the stain to cure for 24 hours, then rinse the slab by brushing on a solution of ½ cup baking soda to 1 gallon of water. Rinse again with plain water. Allow to dry, then use a damp mop to remove any remaining residue. (At this point, the stain will not be the expected color; the full color will be revealed only after the sealer has been applied.)

Once the concrete is dry, use a sprayer, brush, or roller to apply acrylic concrete sealer.

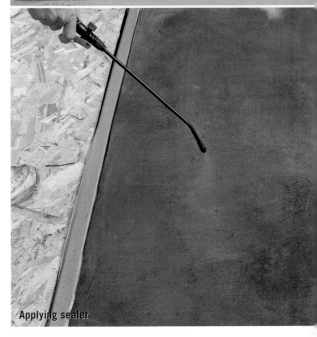

Applying sealer

Right: To create a defined dining area, a ruglike design was etched in the concrete using a masonry saw. Then a simple taupe stain was applied to the entire surface.
Below: On a winding pathway, a paver pattern was stamped into the concrete while it was wet, a technique best left to the pros. Then a base coat of tan-colored stain was applied followed by artful blotches of blue stain.

ADVANCED STAINING TECHNIQUES

If you want to produce a geometric pattern with variously colored sections, there are two basic options:

■ Use a circular saw equipped with a masonry blade to cut a grid of ½-inch-deep lines in the concrete. Mark the lines with a chalk line and use a straight board as a guide when making the cuts. Then apply a different-colored stain to each section using a brush, not a sprayer.

■ Or, first apply a base coat of stain to the entire slab, following the directions on page 79 but omitting the rinsing and the sealer. Once the stain is completely dry, apply strips of vinyl tape to make a design on the slab. Use a brush to apply another color to some of the sections, which will turn a deep, variegated color. Consult with your stain supplier to learn which stains can be combined in this way.

To produce a speckled appearance, apply one coat of stain, allow it to dry, then sprinkle the surface with cornflakes. Lightly spray a dark color over the surface, allow it to dry, then sweep the cornflakes away.

STAINING CONCRETE PAVERS

Pebbles and sand are often exposed in old concrete pavers, so the pavers will not stain to a bright color. However, washing and staining can make them look pleasantly rustic.

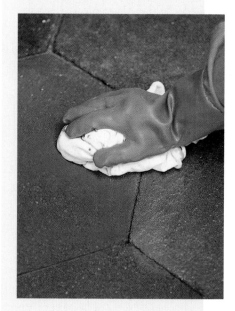

POLYMER COATINGS

Many companies now specialize in covering existing concrete with a polymer-reinforced product that can be colored and stamped or tooled to produce an attractive appearance and a rock-solid surface. These products are generally not available to homeowners and require special tools and techniques to apply. While the cost for adding a polymer coating will likely not be small, doing so certainly beats tearing up the slab and starting over.

Typing "concrete coating" into a search engine will yield a number of companies that apply polymer coatings. Chances are some will have approved contractors in your area. Compare not only prices but warranties before choosing a contractor. If possible, take a look at some of the contractor's work and talk with customers to make sure the work was satisfactory.

PAINTING CONCRETE

This is the simplest way to cover an ugly concrete surface. Paint does not have the nuances of stain, but it does come in a vast array of colors, ranging from muted to wild.

Standard alkyd-based "porch and deck" paint is an inexpensive alternative. For a sturdier surface, choose two-part garage paint or an epoxy paint. Acrylic "stain" penetrates concrete and creates subtle shadings, though not as well as acid stain.

Before applying any type of concrete paint, be sure to clean and rinse the surface thoroughly. To ensure against peeling, apply a primer before applying the paint. Acrylic stain as well as porch and deck paint will last longer if you apply a coat of acrylic sealer over them after they have dried.

Above: Bright painted colors are unusual for a patio but certainly not out of place—especially when they mimic the hues of nearby flowers.
Left: A polymer coating can rejuvenate an existing concrete surface, especially when applied in conjunction with coloring and stamping techniques.

outdoor kitchens

COUNTER MATERIALS Counters are typically made of concrete block, but you can also use steel or wood studs covered with concrete backerboard. You can face the counter with ceramic tile, stone tile, brick, or stucco. The countertop can be made of tile set atop a substructure of concrete backerboard, poured decorative concrete, a granite slab, or a rough stone slab.

If you build with concrete block and other heavy materials, check with your building department to see if you first need to

Left: This barbecue, complete with grill, cooktop, refrigerator, and storage areas with doors, is actually a prefab unit that assembles quickly. Below: A wall of built-in cabinetry, complete with a sink and small refrigerator, nestles under the eaves of this home's exterior. Wood cabinets can survive in a dry climate, or if they are sheltered from rain and snow, as long as they are covered with a solid coat of paint or finish.

Not long ago, outdoor cooking meant a small grill, a tiny working space, an awkward picnic table, and numerous trips to and from the house. Increasingly, homeowners view the space outside their back door as a special outdoor room and want to make it more comfortable and inviting. Manufacturers have responded with an array of products that do just that: large-capacity grills, pizza ovens, cabinets, refrigerators, sinks, overhead protection, and even climate-control features. Many of these products are designed to be permanently built into a counter. See Sunset's *Building Barbecues & Outdoor Kitchens* for design ideas and instructions for building a variety of outdoor kitchens.

A FAIRLY MODEST APPROACH

A built-in propane or charcoal grill set into a 7-foot-long counter with storage below provides a stable cooking appliance and plenty of counter space for preparing the salad and vegetables. To take the simple counter a step or two further, add a raised counter for dining with stools. This arrangement brings family and friends up close with the cook, turning barbecuing and dining into a seamless communal experience.

pour a thick foundation to support the counter.

A number of companies produce doors and drawer units made for outdoor kitchen counters. Be sure to buy them before you build to be certain they will fit. Grills and other appliances also fit into openings in the counter.

THE GRILL The most popular outdoor cooking appliance is a built-in gas grill. For easy installation, use propane gas; the gas tank can fit in the cabinet below. To save money over the long run and to avoid having to change tanks occasionally, hook the grill to a natural gas line. Running a safe gas line may be a major project, however; consult with your building department or a plumber.

The alternative to a gas grill is a charcoal grill. Many people find the taste provided by a charcoal grill far superior to gas, and enjoy the fire-building process as well.

Whichever type of grill you prefer, a host of accessories can greatly enlarge your cooking possibilities. These include rotisseries, infrared cookers, frying griddles that rest on the grill's grate, and a variety of racks designed to hold most any cut of meat or vegetable.

A MORE AMBITIOUS APPROACH

To expand your cooking repertoire and to make food preparation easier, add any of the following:

This Tuscan-style alfresco kitchen boasts hand-hewn wood beams, plaster walls, and a stone-sheathed fireplace. The hearth is elevated to tabletop height, and serves as both a source of warmth and a place to cook pizza. It is flanked by a large soapstone sink on one side and a gas-fired barbecue with a side burner on the other.

A SINK WITH FAUCET If the sink will be near the house, running supply lines may not be too difficult and you may be able to hook into the kitchen drain. In many cases, however, you will need to have the sink drain into the city storm drain or a dry well; consult with a plumber and comply with local plumbing codes. To supply hot water, it is usually easiest to install an instant-hot-water heater under the sink.

REFRIGERATOR Adding a refrigerator is comparatively easy. Build the counter to accommodate an under-counter refrigerator and plug the appliance into a GFCI receptacle.

SIDE BURNER A gas-powered burner or two will allow you to cook pasta and veggies while you grill.

PIZZA OVEN A pizza oven heats to 750°F to produce pizza and breads with crunchy crusts and roasts that are crisp on the outside and tender inside. The oven itself—which can be made of Italian clay or refractory concrete plus fire brick—must be installed and insulated in a large masonry structure. Hire a pro to install one or buy a kit and follow the directions.

building a barbecue counter

This backyard barbecue was built by a homeowner (with assistance from his four young daughters) over the course of six or seven weekends.

The counter was placed against the house just opposite the kitchen sink. This made running the plumbing lines relatively easy; the homeowner was even able to tie the drain directly into the kitchen drain. The existing patio was strong enough to support the unit so a concrete footing did not have to be dug and poured.

This L-shaped structure has a 7-foot-long working counter and a 5½-foot-long eating counter (or bar). The central area, which supports the grill, is made of fire-safe concrete block, and the other areas are framed with wood. Backerboard covers the structure. The counter is then covered with stucco, and the countertop is covered with ceramic tile.

GETTING READY

Purchase the grill, sink, and doors before you begin construction. Plan to build the counter walls to fit.

Draw the outline of the unit on the wall. Then open the wall to gain access to the sink plumbing and work with a plumber to run a code-approved drain line. Either run both cold- and hot-water lines from the inside or run a cold-water line only and install an instant-hot-water heater in the cabinet. Install one GFCI receptacle for the refrigerator and at least one other about 8 inches above the top of the finished counter. Make sure the receptacle will be above the counter's backsplash and in a convenient location for running appliances.

BUILD THE STRUCTURE

Lay concrete blocks to support the grill. To be certain you get the size right, follow the manufacturer's instructions and set the grill in place to make sure it will fit. To lay concrete block, mix mortar (see page 167), spread it with a margin trowel to a thickness of about ½ inch, and set the blocks in the mortar. (For further instructions, see Sunset's *Complete Masonry*.) Where the wood framing will be, firmly attach 2 by 4s to the wall with lag screws or bolts.

Working off the 2 by 4s that are attached to the wall, frame with 2 by 4s or 4 by 4s. Use pressure-treated lumber. Attach the bottom plates to the patio by drilling holes and driving masonry screws. Frame the opening for the door and test that the door will fit. On top, frame for the sink and test that the sink will fit. Frame the countertop so that the backerboard will be supported at least every 12 inches or so.

The dining counter must cantilever out about 15 inches to

make room for diners' legs. Build a double 2-by-4 wall. Construct a counter frame out of 2 by 4s and firmly anchor the frame to the double wall using angle irons and screws. The counter should feel firm when you push down on it at the outside corner.

COVER WITH BACKERBOARD

Use a backerboard knife or a utility knife to cut pieces of ½-inch concrete backerboard to fit both the counter sides and the countertops. Attach the backerboard to the wood studs by driving backerboard screws; attach to the concrete block using thinset mortar. As you work, test again to make sure that the doors, sink, and grill will fit. At the backerboard joints, apply fiberglass mesh tape and cover the tape with a coating of thinset mortar.

Apply waterproof tile backing to cover both countertops. Cut the backing with a utility knife and use thinset mortar to hold it in place.

Apply stucco to the visible sides of the counter (see pages 86–87).

SET THE TILES

See pages 172–75 for instructions on applying tiles. Lay the tiles in a dry run on the counters; you may need to adjust the layout in order to avoid having an unattractive row of very thin tiles at one edge. Carefully plan how you will tile the edges and corners. Using a wet saw or a snap cutter, cut as many tiles as possible.

Once you are satisfied with the layout, mix a batch of latex- or polymer-reinforced thinset mortar and set the tiles. Use plastic spacers if the tiles are regularly sized; carefully eyeball the layout if the tiles are irregular. To keep the edge tiles from sliding down before the mortar dries, hold them in place with pieces of masking tape.

Apply grout and wipe clean. Install the doors, sink, and grill by setting them in and driving screws as indicated. Apply caulk to the door flanges and the sink flanges as you set them in to make them watertight. Hook up the plumbing for the sink and the gas line or propane tank for the grill. Plug in the refrigerator.

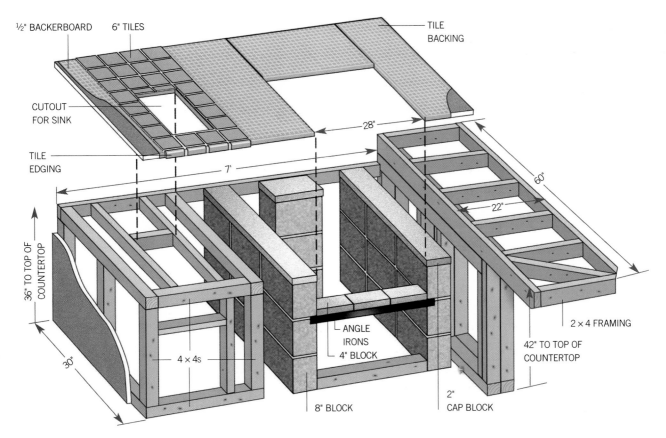

½" BACKERBOARD   6" TILES   TILE BACKING
CUTOUT FOR SINK
TILE EDGING
28"
7'
60"
22"
36" TO TOP OF COUNTERTOP
30"
4 × 4s
ANGLE IRONS
4" BLOCK
8" BLOCK
2" CAP BLOCK
2 × 4 FRAMING
42" TO TOP OF COUNTERTOP

covering a barbecue counter with stucco

Left uncolored, stucco has a soft, mellow appearance. It can also be tinted before you apply it, or painted after it has dried.

It will take a couple of hours to get the hang of stuccoing. Fortunately, the base coat—which you install at the beginning of your learning curve—will be covered up. Before applying the finish coat, practice on a vertical piece of plywood or on an obscure portion of the wall. That way, when you start applying the final coat to a visible area, you will be practiced enough to produce a surface that is consistent in appearance.

1 Apply the Base Coat

Pour half a bag of dry stucco base-coat mix into a wheelbarrow. Add water and mix with a mason's hoe or a garden hoe to produce a pasty consistency. The stucco should be just firm enough to hold its shape when you pick it up with a trowel. Place a shovelful of stucco on a mason's hawk (as shown) or a piece of plywood. Hold the hawk against the wall as you work, so you can catch any drips. Scoop up the stucco with a straight finishing trowel and slather it onto the wall, all the time pressing it into place. Aim at a coat that has a uniform thickness of ⅜ inch.

2 Scarify

The base coat, also called the "scratch coat," gets roughed up to ensure the next coats will stick. Comb the surface with a scarifying tool or a piece of 1 by 2 with nails poking through, as shown. Work to produce indentations without raising large crumbs. For maximum strength, regularly spray with a fine mist of water to ensure that the base coat cures slowly—ideally, for two days.

3 Finish Coat

Mix stucco for the finish coat using the same method you used for the base coat, except make the mix slightly wetter. If you buy white stucco finish, you can mix it with dry colorant for long-lasting color. Apply the finish coat as you applied the base coat. Aim for a surface that is fairly smooth and free of streaks made by the trowel.

4 Create a Texture

See right for some stucco texture possibilities. To make a swirled texture as shown here, set the blade of a masonry trowel in the stucco and rotate it to create about half of a circle. Make subsequent swirls that overlap each other by roughly the same amount. Avoid having arcs that appear to be stacked on top of each other.

TEXTURE OPTIONS

Whichever technique you choose, find a pattern that comes naturally to you so that you can easily repeat it.

- To make a spatter coat, dip a whisk broom in the stucco and shake it toward the wall. Aim for a pattern that evenly distributes large and small globs. It may help to add a bit of water to the stucco that gets spattered.

- Perhaps the easiest pattern is made by brushing the stucco lightly with a mason's brush. You may choose overlapping rainbowlike swirls, as shown. Or, paint with short strokes that run in three or four directions. Brush while the stucco is still wet. If the brush starts to leave globs, rinse it off and start again.

- To make a knockdown texture, spatter the wall as shown in the top photo. Wait about 15 minutes (depending on the humidity) and then run a trowel very lightly over the surface to flatten some, but not all, of the spatters. Many people find that a rounded pool trowel, as shown, is easier to work with than a square-cornered trowel.

Spatter coat

Brush strokes

Knockdown texture

firepits

A firepit made of rough stones that are stacked and mortared is at home in this rustic setting.

An above-ground firepit, surrounded by a low (18–24 inches tall) masonry wall, is the most elaborate setup. But it is a permanent garden element, handsome and useful whether or not a fire is going. When topped with a wide ledge, the wall provides seating and a perfect perch for roasting marshmallows.

An in-ground firepit captures the magic of wilderness campfires. It can be as casual as a hole in the ground

There's something hypnotic about an open fire; people are naturally drawn to the warm glow. You don't have to travel to a camping site to relax around a flickering fire— you can bring a firepit into your own backyard. With its crackling flames and popping sparks, a firepit is sure to become a focal point for an enjoyable post-dinner evening under the stars.

Because masonry materials, which firepits are made of, are by nature nonflammable, there's a good chance you can find a safe place for a firepit on or near your patio. Of course, you will need to keep it well away from overhanging branches or any wooden structures so that flames and sparks can't start an unwanted fire.

A firepit is basically a hole in the ground with a decorative stone or brick ring constructed around it. Building one is a simple masonry project. If you want a gas-powered fire or a gas log lighter, you will need to run a gas line into the pit.

surrounded by rocks or lined with bricks or stones for a more finished look.

You can also buy a metal fireplace; simply place it in a safe spot on a nonflammable surface and build a fire.

Kids will clamor to roast hot dogs or marshmallows over an open fire. But a firepit can be used for serious cooking as well. Harkening back to the earliest cooking fires, it can be fitted out with spits, tripods, cooking grates, and rotisseries. Of course, cooking with such equipment is less convenient and a bit more sweaty than cooking on a standard grill, but many people enjoy the more rustic experience.

Above: Creating your own back-yard firepit can be as simple as digging a hole and lining it with rocks or bricks. Add wood and fire and you're ready for a campfire experience. *Left:* A simple metal wood-burning firepit safely set on a stone patio adds a glow of warmth to the seating area.

planning for
a new patio

A well-thought-out patio is not only a delight to the eye; it is sized and shaped to comfortably accommodate all the furniture and activities that make outdoor living a joy. Whether you want to install a small grouping of flagstones or a spacious paver patio, it pays to plan carefully. This chapter guides you through the entire planning process, from choosing materials and tools to creating working drawings.

patio design samples

To help get your creative juices flowing, we show four examples of successful patio designs. In all these plans, you will see that the patio must be considered in relation to the rest of the yard. Trees, flowers, the lawn, and vertical structures all may frame the patio, and the patio itself should be oriented to help you enjoy the scenery.

A PATIO PATH

What can you do with a long, narrow area on the side of your house? That's the question that confronted the owner of this property when, after converting her garage into a home office, she needed to landscape what had been a driveway. The solution was to transform a tight-feeling rectangle into a wide, flowing path. Slabs of bluish-gray Mariposa flagstones meander on either side of the area, moving apart and then together, creating separate spaces that are wide enough to act like small patios. A low red wall at one ends adds visual drama and helps to define the space.

The patio itself is made of crushed stone—a form of decomposed granite often referred to as "gold granite fines." This "loose" material is hard enough to be swept and yet allows rainwater to seep right through—a necessary condition in a narrow space with little drainage.

Lush plantings, including low ground covers, small trees and bushes, and vines that climb on screens and trellises, complete the appearance of a flowing river and make the space feel ample rather than cramped.

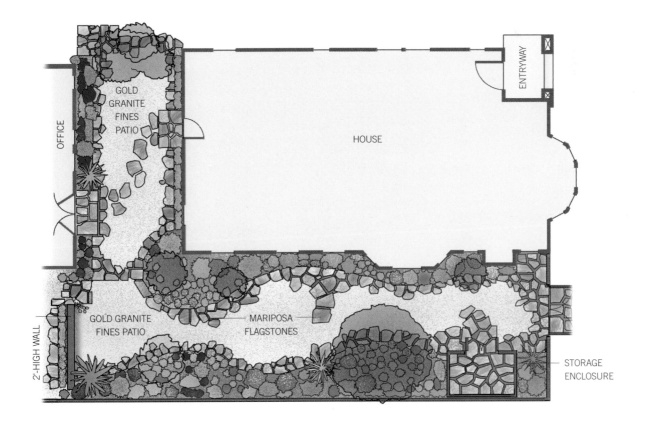

OFFICE

GOLD GRANITE FINES PATIO

HOUSE

ENTRYWAY

2'-HIGH WALL

GOLD GRANITE FINES PATIO

MARIPOSA FLAGSTONES

STORAGE ENCLOSURE

ELEGANT YET INVITING BLUESTONE

This patio certainly shows off its spacious dimensions, but, because it was carefully shaped and surrounded with plantings, it also optimizes its usefulness as a place to gather and relax with friends.

There are actually two patios. The upper patio is a wide walkway, convenient to the kitchen, with an area large enough for a modest cooking center. The shape incorporates both curved and straight lines to create a sophisticated profile. Notice that the curved benches match the curves of the patio.

The lower patio is much larger and shaped like the prow of a ship facing the yard. Because of its relation to adjacent paths, the patio provides three distinct conversation and lounging areas: to the left, a small nook with two chairs and a coffee table well sheltered by a high hedge and some trees; to the right, a single bench somewhat less sheltered but with a view of the yard; and, in the middle, a larger sun-receiving area visible from the patio above and open to the yard on the other side.

Both patios are made of magnificent bluestone slabs; their blue, gray, and rose tones create a subtle patchwork effect. In slanting light, these colors make the lush greens and hot flower shades seem cooler, making this a very relaxing place to be.

The upper patio is located just outside the living room doors, but is easily accessed from the kitchen via a deck. It commands a view of the large lower patio and the yard beyond.

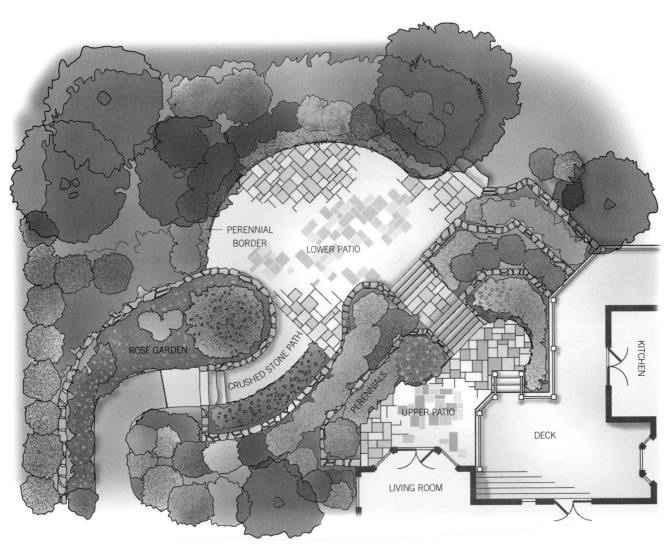

PERENNIAL BORDER

LOWER PATIO

ROSE GARDEN

CRUSHED STONE PATH

PERENNIALS

UPPER PATIO

KITCHEN

DECK

LIVING ROOM

PEACEFUL RETREAT

This patio and garden has no areas for cooking or dining; those activities take place on the deck that abuts the house. Its purpose, however, is just as useful: to provide a quiet place to stroll amid the foliage and to sit next to the pool and commune with the fish.

The overall plan makes a small, awkwardly shaped site seem spacious. This goal was accomplished partly by using tall plantings around the perimeter that obscure the fact that the neighbors' yard is only a few feet away. Plantings are at other levels, too, from the lily pads in the water to the raised beds to the natural slopes on the perimeter, adding to the sense that this is a natural place. A small pond with a distinctive shape also generates visual interest that makes the space feel more than ample.

The design recycled or barely modified features that were already on site. The pond is a former spa to which a straight channel, called a "rill," was added. The yard's original berms (little hills) were not razed but were converted into raised beds.

The pond surround is paved with Arizona flagstone; the rest of the patio is made of decomposed granite. The two paving materials are close in color so they do not draw attention to themselves and allow the plants to shine.

Though it is not immediately apparent, a good deal of seating is actually available. Many of the flat stones used to create planting beds are at the right height for sitting, providing a variety of pleasant places to relax and converse.

Decorative elements in the garden combine old Spanish style with an eclectic California look. At the entrance, a large rustic gate with an overhead beam, painted a dramatic blue, makes for a theatrical screen that completes the picture.

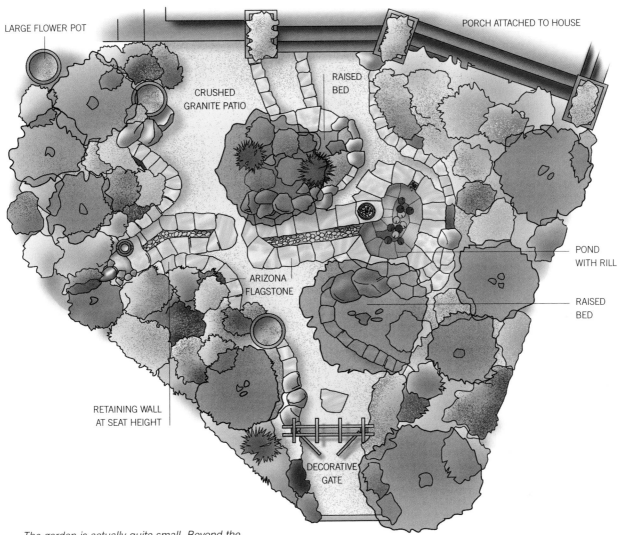

LARGE FLOWER POT

PORCH ATTACHED TO HOUSE

CRUSHED
GRANITE PATIO

RAISED
BED

ARIZONA
FLAGSTONE

POND
WITH RILL

RAISED
BED

RETAINING WALL
AT SEAT HEIGHT

DECORATIVE
GATE

*The garden is actually quite small. Beyond the
steps (or are they seats?) near the pond you can see
the gate, which abuts the neighbor's driveway.*

PATIO WITH A VIEW

You don't need to overlook the Grand Canyon in order to have a stunning view; a moderately large yard can be just as pleasing if you plan carefully. This patio is large enough for normal cooking and dining uses, but it also encourages a view toward a nicely arranged and open yard.

As long as you keep the sight lines open, your yard doesn't need to be elevated to produce a view. In this case, the patio is less than 2 feet above the lawn it abuts. But the spacious grass area slopes gently downward away from the house, bringing into view the yard's small plantings, a casita, and an herb garden beyond. Larger trees and bushes located to the side don't inhibit the view.

The pattern on the patchwork patio surface would have to be called random, but there was indeed a method to the madness. Bricks of various colors were combined with odd-shaped flag-stones. The bricks run in several directions but generally describe a path through the patio. When they reach the steps, they are regular and orderly. Forming an arrangement like this requires a good deal of planning and patience to produce an effect that is artistic rather than sloppy.

The potted plants placed on the patio near the steps establish a feeling of being enclosed without getting in the way of the attractive view.

Standing on the patchwork-style patio you can look out onto the brick-edged lawn and the casita beyond. A long sweep of edging, composed of the same bricks that are used on the patio, separates the lawn from the perennial planting bed.

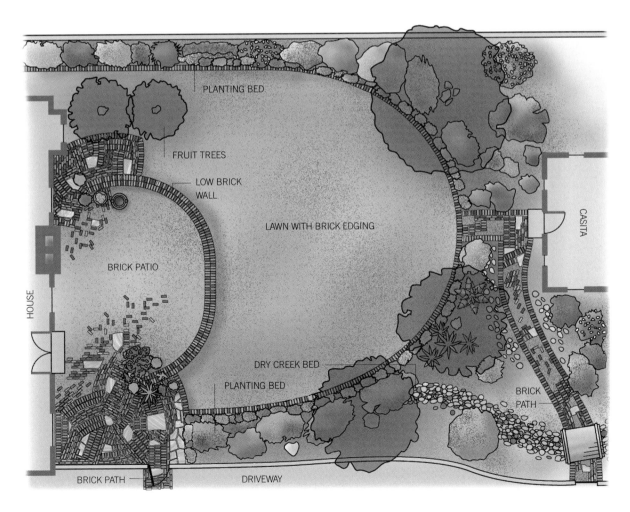

PLANTING BED

FRUIT TREES

LOW BRICK WALL

LAWN WITH BRICK EDGING

BRICK PATIO

HOUSE

CASITA

DRY CREEK BED

PLANTING BED

BRICK PATH

BRICK PATH

DRIVEWAY

flagstone

Stone pavers offer the warmth of a natural material and are generally very durable. The term "flagstone" refers to any flat stone of irregular shape, usually from ¾ to 3 inches thick. Flagstone works in almost any setting: its natural, unfinished look blends well with plants, its subdued colors—buff, yellow, brownish-red, and gray—add warmth to a patio, and its irregularly shaped slabs contribute a pleasing texture.

Smooth flagstones can form a fairly formal surface, especially if they are carefully cut so that the joints between them are consistent in width and filled with mortar. Rougher flagstones with variable joints filled with soil or sand are more casual in appearance.

Flagstone is usually made by splitting rather than cutting natural stone, giving it its characteristic rough surface, which may be bumpy, pitted, or composed of different mesalike planes. If you plan to frequently use chairs and tables, wheelchairs, or wheeled toys on the patio, make

Flagstones carefully mortared onto a concrete slab can form a surface that is as smooth as a brick patio. Notice that some of the stone edges are cut fairly straight, while others have more natural contours.

sure that the flagstone surface isn't too rough or uneven.

The availability of different types, shapes, sizes, and colors of flagstone depends on where you live. Different types also have different features: marble and granite have very hard surfaces, making them the easiest to keep clean; limestone and sandstone are more porous; slate falls somewhere in between.

IRISH LINEN FLAGSTONE

MARIPOSA SLATE

BUFF ARIZONA FLAGSTONE

THREE RIVERS FLAGSTONE

BOUQUET CANYON FLAGSTONE

Marble and granite are the most difficult to cut by hand; limestone is almost as hard. Some types of slate are very hard while others crack easily. Sandstone is easy to cut but also cracks easily, so be sure it is well supported when you lay it.

Most flagstones are strong enough to be set directly in soil; this is one of the easiest ways to build a patio (see pages 121–23). However, stones labeled "veneer" are probably not thick enough to be installed this way. Flagstones can also be set in sand, the way pavers are set for a paver patio (pages 153–54); in dabs of mortar (pages 132–33); or in mortar atop a concrete slab (pages 168–71).

Flagstones can be casually strewn near a bench to make for a casual reading area (below) or precisely cut to create intricate grout lines (right).

Stones that are roughly cut into rectangles or other shapes are sometimes called cobblestones or "cobbles." You can use them to form a small patio or to create edgings or accents.

GRANITE COBBLESTONES

ROCKY MOUNTAIN FLATS

CARAMEL SWIRL
THIN VENEER

CRANBERRY
THIN VENEER

SUNSET SILVER
QUARTZ SLATE

brick

Natural brick, made by firing clay in a kiln, provides a handsome surface that blends with nearly any architectural style and seems at home in almost any setting. It is more expensive than concrete pavers (see pages 102–3), but many people find its natural beauty well worth the extra cost.

If you live in an area with freezing winters, be sure to buy bricks made specifically for paving (often rated "MX"). Common bricks, bricks with two or three holes, and other bricks that are made for walls rather than patios (often rated "SX") may crack or flake during freeze-thaw cycles. If you do use wall bricks for paving, apply a coat of acrylic sealer every year or two so they don't soak up water.

Bricks that are often exposed to moisture may develop a white-colored stain called efflorescence. Some people appreciate the rustic look of this imperfection, but if you do not, it can be washed away with a detergent or with a pressure-washer. Bricks that are laid in very moist, heavily shaded areas can become slick with algae-like growth, which can be cleaned away with a mild bleach solution; treat mold the same way.

Two types of brick—a fairly formal paving brick and a lighter-colored common brick—are combined in an unusual way to define a dining area. Bricks of various sizes and shapes are carefully arranged to form what are nearly, but not quite, regular patterns. To form the curved line where the two types of brick meet, a cutoff saw was used to cut the formal bricks (see page 157); then common bricks were cut separately to fit.

Bricks come in a wide variety of colors, textures, and shapes. You can combine several types in a single patio, but first check that all the bricks are exactly the same size. "Clinkers" have irregularities and dark spots produced by overburning in the kiln, and provide a rough, cobblestone appearance. "Face bricks" are usually used for walls because of their hard, smooth surface; they are suitable only for accents or edgings on a patio. "Frogged" bricks have old-fashioned indentations bearing the name of the manufacturer; they make for interesting accents. Faux "used" bricks are often actually concrete pavers made to look like old common bricks—complete with fake efflorescence.

BRICK PAVER PATTERNS

A brick patio can harmonize with almost any design style, thanks in large part to the range of patterns in which the bricks can be laid. A simple pattern such as running bond has a timeless, understated look. A more intricate pattern can make the patio surface a focal point. A basketweave pattern can actually be easier to install than running bond, because you may not have to cut any bricks. See pages 153–58 for instructions on installing these patterns.

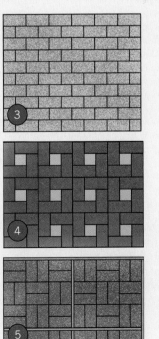

1. 45-DEGREE HERRINGBONE
2. 90-DEGREE HERRINGBONE
3. RUNNING BOND
4. PINWHEEL
5. BASKETWEAVE WITH 2 × 4 GRID

concrete pavers

Once limited to gray or pinkish colors, concrete pavers now come in an array of attractive colors and shapes. Though some people feel they lack the subtle charm of natural brick, concrete pavers are extremely durable and inexpensive, making them a great value.

Rectangular concrete pavers are installed much like bricks and can be arranged in the same patterns (see page 101). "Interlocking" concrete pavers fit together like puzzle pieces. They may include only one shape or two or three shapes. Both interlocking and noninterlocking rectangular pavers make very stable patios.

All concrete pavers are difficult to cut by hand; use a masonry saw (see pages 148–49) to cut them. They can be set in sand (pages 150–54) or laid in mortar atop a concrete slab (pages 178–79).

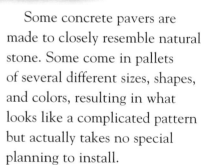

Some concrete pavers are made to closely resemble natural stone. Some come in pallets of several different sizes, shapes, and colors, resulting in what looks like a complicated pattern but actually takes no special planning to install.

You can also buy circular or fan-shaped concrete paver ensembles, which typically use five or six different shapes. The manufacturer's instructions will show you which pavers go where.

Large rust-colored pavers are each framed with small, square pavers. In a design like this, it is important that the small pavers be the same thickness as the large ones.

Left: If you purchase pavers of various sizes and shapes made to work together to form circles, it is easy to improvise an added curvy flourish; you may need to custom cut several pavers to do so. *Below:* It's hard to tell the difference between these concrete pavers and natural cut stones.

Large pavers—as wide as 24 inches—enable you to quickly create a patio surface. You can set them in soil, sand, or dabs of mortar (see pages 132–33). Because they are so heavy, no edging is needed to keep them in place.

Turf blocks handle traffic while retaining and protecting grass or crevice plants. Grassy walkways and even driveways made with turf block are both charming and durable.

Left: Turf block is set in a flagstone patio, allowing strips of grass to grow. *Below:* Modular pavers—which are easily laid in various patterns—come in a variety of shapes and sizes.

tile

Tile looks as great indoors as out, so it's a good material to use on room surfaces as well as adjacent patios. Letting tile flow outdoors creates a spacious feeling, especially during warm weather when connecting doors are open. The seemingly unbroken expanse of floor beckons you and your guests to enjoy the patio.

CERAMIC TILE

Ceramic tile is typically set in mortar on a solid concrete slab. There are four practical considerations to keep in mind when choosing tile for a patio.

- The tile must be strong enough to support weight; wall tiles and other soft tiles will crack when used for an outdoor floor.
- It must be able to survive winters in your area. Porous tile will soak up water and crack when the water freezes. Applying a sealer may prevent this in some cases, but consult with a tile supplier to make sure that the tiles you choose will winter well.
- It must not be slippery; glazed ceramic tile is often slippery when wet. Some tiles with bumpy surfaces offer slip resistance.
- The tile should be easy to keep clean. Porous tiles will be difficult to keep clean unless you regularly apply acrylic sealer.

Terra-cotta tile comes in warm brown and red hues. Some terra-cotta tiles are precisely shaped, while others, such as Mexican Saltillos, have somewhat irregular shapes. Saltillos are available in glazed or unglazed versions. One popular look combines terra-cotta tiles with some small colored accent tiles.

Glazed ceramic tile comes in most every color imaginable. Some types will survive harsh winters. Quarry tile is unglazed but very hard and dense, making it both skid resistant and able to survive freezing weather. Colors are limited, however, to grays and beiges. Porcelain tile comes in a vast array of colors and textures; it can reproduce the look of ceramic, stone, and even marble. Porcelain tile is durable in all sorts of weather and very resistant to staining.

STONE TILE

Some stone tiles are cut as precisely as ceramic tile while others vary slightly in thickness and width. Most stone tiles should be set in a bed of mortar atop a concrete slab. Thicker and stronger types can be set in sand like bricks or concrete pavers.

Like flagstones (see pages 98–99), stone tiles vary in porosity, strength, and color. Consult with your tile supplier to be sure the stone tiles you choose will survive in your situation. Coat them with acrylic sealer to protect them from staining.

Slate tiles are now available from all over the world, including Africa, India, and Mexico. Some are consistently grayish or ruddy while others exhibit variable colors, including veins of silver and rust. Some types are very hard and durable while others are easily cracked.

Bluestone, once sold only on the East Coast, is now available through much of the country. Some types have a consistent blue-gray color; others have streaks of ochre, rust, green, or purple. Bluestone is available in various thicknesses. "Tread stock" is thick and strong enough to be used as a step with minimal support.

Above: Slate tiles typically come in several complementary hues that produce a pleasing patchwork effect. **Left:** Tumbled marble tiles are inlaid with strips of pebble mosaics to add interest. Stone tiles like these must be sealed or they will easily soak up stains.

gravel and pebbles

For economy, good drainage, and ease of installation, consider installing loose materials such as gravel, crushed rock, or pebbles. Because they're natural, they go well with almost any paving material. Gravel generally refers to sharp-edged stones while pebbles have smooth, rounded edges. Crushed rock is made of very small, sharp stones. Crushed rock and small-stoned gravel can form a surprisingly firm and stable surface, though a few stones will escape when walked on. Pebbles and large-stoned gravel surfaces are more loose and therefore not suited for high-traffic areas. Gravels and pebbles are often named for the regions where they were quarried.

Gravel and pebbles can be raked into patterns or set into decorative openings in other paving materials. Or you can install dividers made of wood or other edgings and fill each section with a different type of gravel or pebbles.

A loose-material patio may be difficult to keep clean when leaves fall on it. A leaf blower will work well if you catch the leaves when they are dry.

Loose materials are ideal for installation around a tree whose roots grow near the surface; a standard patio would be heaved upward unattractively. However, limestone gravel will leach minerals into the soil that may be harmful to trees, so consult with a nursery or install other types of gravel or pebbles.

When choosing a loose material, consider color, sheen, texture, and size. You may want to take home small bags as color swatches. Gravel and pebbles often look very different when wet, so spray on some water to see how that will look.

Above: *This gravel is carefully laid at a level just below the large edging stones for a patio that is surprisingly stable and easy to maintain.*

ADOBE PAVERS

With its massive form and warm, earthy color, adobe creates a friendly, informal tone the way few other paving materials can. Adobe looks best when used in generous, open yards. Some types are irregular in shape while others are manufactured with the precision of bricks. Like brick and concrete pavers, adobe is generally laid in sand to form a patio. Because the blocks are massive—two common sizes are 4 by 8 by 8 and 4 by 8 by 16—a patio can be created quickly.

Adobe is easy to find only in the Southwest, but is increasingly available in other areas. A brickyard or stone yard may be able to order some for you. Today's adobe blocks are stabilized with Portland cement or asphalt emulsion, making them durable in almost any climate.

planning for drainage

I f you follow the instructions in this book and install a patio that is consistently sloped away from the house at a rate of $\frac{1}{4}$ inch per running foot, the patio itself will not develop puddles. However, water will run to the edges of the patio, which can create wet spots. Most drainage problems can be addressed after the patio is installed, but it is a good idea to think about drainage ahead of time. If you cannot slope the patio away from the house, you must install a drainage system before laying the pavers (see page 109).

Also consider if rainwater will be able to drain through paver joints. When a patio has wide sand- or soil-filled joints between pavers, rainwater can seep down through them. However, a standard sand-laid patio with tight joints will let very little water seep through.

PERIMETER TRENCHES

If you find occasional small puddles forming at the edge of your patio after a rainfall, you can usually solve the problem by digging a trench about 8 inches deep and 16 inches wide and filling it with a combination of mulch and well-drained soil. Dress it up by adding some decorative shrubs or flowers.

Smooth, black pebbles not only look great around a patio, they also allow water to seep through into the ground, eliminating puddles.

If the problem is a bit more severe—say, you have small puddles after a moderate rain—then dig a trench 12 inches deep and 16 inches wide and fill it with gravel or pebbles. If you have a larger problem—large puddles that remain for a day or two before drying up—lay a perforated drainpipe in the trench, sloped so that it carries water away (see

below). You can place the drainpipe so that it meanders through the lawn; water will trickle out through the perforations. Or you can set it so that it pokes through to daylight at a hillside or ends in a dry well (see page 109). The drainpipe must slope downward consistently at a rate of about $\frac{1}{4}$ inch per running foot. If you need to run the pipe over a distance longer than 50 feet or so, or if you are unsure how to maintain the slope, you should probably hire a landscaping contractor who can do the work for you.

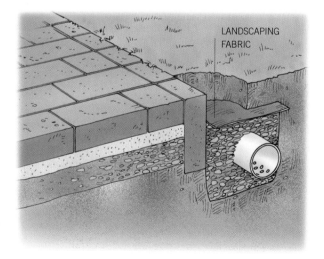

LANDSCAPING FABRIC

DRAINING INTO A DRY WELL

If you have lots of water to drain, or if there is no good place to run the drainpipe, run the pipe into a dry well, which is simply a large hole filled with gravel. A dry well about 3 feet wide and 3 feet deep will solve most problems: water will slowly percolate into the surrounding soil. To make a dry well, dig a hole and run sloped drainpipe into it. Next, fill the hole with coarse gravel or pebbles—not compactible gravel. Then, cover the hole with three layers of landscaping fabric and top that with soil and sod.

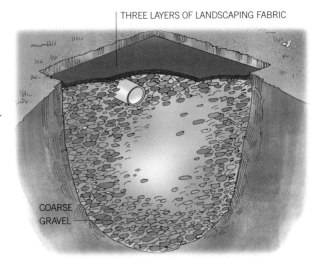

THREE LAYERS OF LANDSCAPING FABRIC

COARSE GRAVEL

CATCH BASIN

If your site does not allow you to slope the patio away from the house, you may need a central catch basin. This must be installed before you lay pavers. Slope the excavation so that water will run to a spot that's near the middle of the patio (see below). At that spot, dig a hole and install a cylindrical or rectangular catch basin, available at brickyards or home centers. Position it so that the basin's grate is just below the level of the surrounding pavers. From the catch basin, run solid (not perforated) drainpipe at a slope, to carry water away from the patio. Once the pipe reaches the edge of the patio, switch to perforated pipe and run it around the yard or to a dry well.

The grate will catch leaves and other large objects that could clog the pipe. You may occasionally need to sweep the grate clean so that water can flow through it.

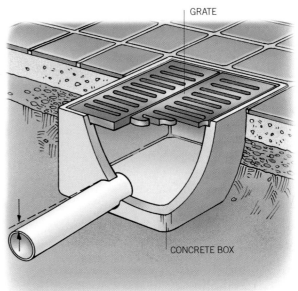

GRATE

CONCRETE BOX

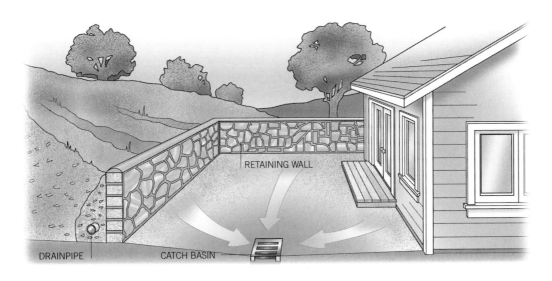

RETAINING WALL

DRAINPIPE

CATCH BASIN

coping with the weather

If you know what to expect from the weather in your area, you can plan a patio that you can enjoy over the longest possible season, and one that will take advantage of the weather tendencies on your property. You're probably already familiar with your climate's benefits and hazards, but to obtain more scientific information, type "climate" plus the name of your town and/or state into a search engine. Check the Web sites indicated for relevant data about average temperatures, precipitation, and sunrises and sunsets.

TRACKING THE SUN

A patio's exposure to the sun is one of the most important factors in your enjoyment of the space. Knowing the sun's path over your property may prompt you to adjust the site of your proposed patio, extend its dimensions, or change its design in order to add weeks or even months of sun or shade to your outdoor room. Often you can moderate the effects of the sun with the addition of an overhead (see pages 39–45).

All other factors being equal, a patio that faces north receives less sun than one that faces south. A patio on the east side is relatively cool, because it receives only morning sun. One that faces west receives sunlight in the mid-afternoon, which could make it very hot. In addition, late afternoon sun often creates a harsh glare. If you live in a hot area, you will probably want to situate your patio on the cooler sides: east and north. In a cooler climate, south and west orientations may be preferable.

Also consider the sun's path during the year (see below). As the sun passes over your house, it makes an arc that changes a little bit every day, becoming higher in summer and lower in winter. Changes in the sun's path give us longer days in summer and shorter days in winter, and they also alter sun and shade patterns on your patio. Find your location on the map (left) and then refer to the accompanying chart for sun angles and hours of daylight that your property receives.

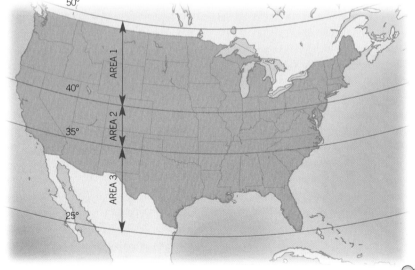

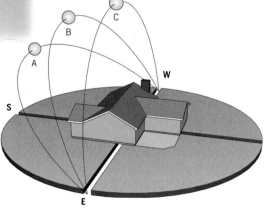

THE SUN IN YOUR YARD

SEASONAL SUN ANGLES	SUN'S POSITION/HOURS OF DAYLIGHT (SEE MAP ABOVE)		
SEASON/DATE	AREA 1	AREA 2	AREA 3
A) Noon, 12/21	21°/8 hrs.	29°/9 hrs.	37°/10 hrs.
B) Noon, 3/21 & 9/21	45°/12 hrs.	53°/12 hrs.	60°/12 hrs.
C) Noon, 6/21	69°/16 hrs.	76°/15 hrs.	83°/14 hrs.

TAMING THE WIND

Observe the wind patterns around your house and over your lot. Too much wind blowing across your patio on a cool day can be just as unpleasant as no breeze at all on a hot day. Evaluating the wind patterns will help you discover how to control (or encourage) the wind with fences, screens, or plants.

Three different kinds of wind can affect your site: annual prevailing winds, localized seasonal breezes (daily, late afternoon, or summer), and occasional high-velocity winds generated by storms. You can determine the prevailing winds in your neighborhood by watching flags or leaves on trees, but chances are the prevailing winds around your home are different. Wind flows like water, spilling over obstacles, breaking into currents, eddying and twisting.

A solid vertical barrier, such as a solid fence, is not necessarily the most effective wind barrier. In general, it will provide great protection for only a small area—roughly, the same distance as the height of the fence. Farther away, wind will swirl downward onto the patio. A barrier with openings, such as a fence made with lattice or spaced pickets or a series of shrubs, will diffuse rather than block the wind and provide more even protection for a larger area.

UNDERSTANDING MICROCLIMATES

Shade and breeze can dramatically modify how you experience your area's temperature and humidity. On any patio, nearby buildings, trees, shrubs, and overhead structures create microclimates, meaning that the conditions on your patio may be very different from those on a neighbor's patio. One area of your patio may also feel very different from another area.

In addition to shade and wind barriers, keep in mind that certain materials reflect sun and/or heat better than others. Light-colored masonry paving and walls are great at spreading sun and heat, but they can be uncomfortably bright. Beige pavers and siding, as well as wood surfaces, are usually cooler. Dark masonry materials retain heat longer, warming your patio in the evening. Well-placed deciduous trees shelter a patio in summer yet allow welcome rays to penetrate in late autumn and winter.

Above: A simple lattice screen with climbing plants can provide serious shelter from wind. *Below:* This small yard has several microclimates. Some parts are shaded most of the day, others are in nearly constant sun. The plants near the wall are more protected from wind. Plants near the pool receive more moisture.

drawing a plan

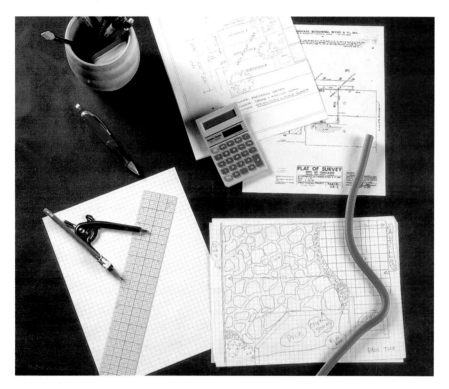

You've probably already begun the design process by thinking about your ideal patio, gathering ideas from magazines, and checking out patios in your neighborhood. Also spend some time with the first chapter of this book and perhaps take a look at Sunset's *Ideas for Great Patios & Decks*.

You should also ask family members what they would like to have and do in the backyard. At the top of the list may be a large space for sit-down entertaining at a single table or scattered sites for small groups to gather. A secluded spot for lounging, a space for children's play (perhaps in plain view from the kitchen), or a gardening center may also be on the list.

MAPPING THE YARD

Start by making a base map of your yard. If you have a deed map or a surveyor's plot of survey, photocopy it and use it as a base. Measure as precisely as you can; "guesstimates" or outright errors can result in disappointments later when, for example, you find that your new patio is in shade when you most want to use it for sun-loving activities.

Draw your base map on a large sheet of graph paper. Useful drawing tools include a pencil with a good eraser, a compass, a clear lined draftsman's ruler for easily drawing parallel lines, a calculator, and a curved-line guide (all of which are shown in the photo above).

To measure the landscape, use either a 50- or 100-foot tape measure. Draw your base map directly on graph paper or on tracing paper placed over graph paper. First measure and draw the outlines of the relevant portion of your property. Show the portion of the house that will abut the patio. Draw an arrow indicating north.

Draw in all trees, indicating measurements not of the trunks but the canopy provided by the branches and leaves. Then add shrubs, flower or vegetable beds, and other plantings. If you know where future plantings will go, include those as well. Indicate any downspouts and other drainage features. If the lawn slopes, indicate where and how steeply. Note areas that are particularly shady or sunny. If there is an attractive view you would like to emphasize, make note of that as well.

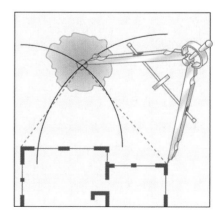

To precisely locate a tree or other feature, triangulate: measure from two widely spaced fixed points to the feature. Working from scale, use a compass to draw two arcs; the intersection of the arcs marks the exact spot.

MAKING A BUBBLE PLAN

Make five or six photocopies of the base plan and work on them to produce a bubble plan that generally indicates where you would like to put what. Feel free to experiment at this point; you can always throw out ideas that don't work. Sketch in a few "bubbles"—rough circles or ovals that represent the approximate locations and sizes of each use area (see right).

As you draw, concentrate on logical placement and juxtaposition. Are you locating a children's play area in full view of your living area? Is the cooking area convenient to the kitchen? Are the attractive views—both from inside the house and the patio—preserved?

PLANNING THE USE AREAS

To ensure that there is ample room for all your activities—cooking, dining, lounging, conversing, playing—think of your outdoor living space in terms of use areas that are joined by paths. Here are some general guidelines:

- A lounge chair or hammock with a small end table needs a space about 4 by 8 feet.
- A barbecue area needs room for at least one small preparation table plus the barbecue unit. A 6-by-8-foot space will accommodate a cook with one or two "helpers."

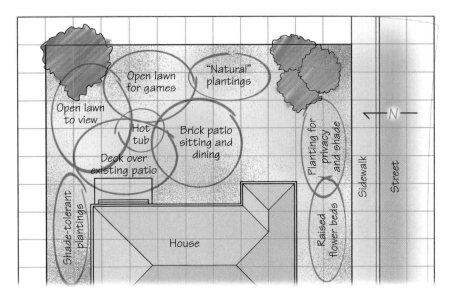

- To calculate a dining area, measure the table and add 3 to 4 feet on all sides for chair space. A typical round or square table will require an area 10 to 12 feet square. A rectangular table for eight will need an area 10 to 12 feet by 16 to 18 feet.
- Be sure to include room for the pathways that lead from one area to another. A 3-foot-wide path comfortably accommodates light traffic.

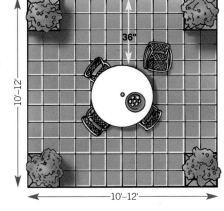

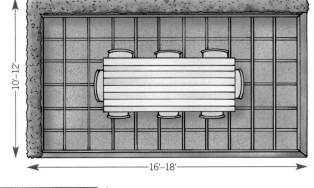

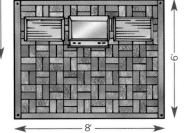

113

MAKING THE DRAWINGS

Time spent drawing and redrawing plans will likely pay for itself in work saved later. A set of detailed and accurate plans will help you execute your design with fewer mistakes. The process of drawing plans helps you think through the building process so that you can spot and solve problems ahead of time. See pages 90–97 for examples of patio designs with drawings.

WORKING IN MODULES Many people find it helpful to design in a modular way. Start with a single unit of space—usually, a square or a rectangle— and repeat that shape several times in the overall plan. Using uniform design units enables you to be more exact in planning and gives a sense of order to your design. You'll also find modules helpful when estimating materials—just figure the materials needed for one module, then tally the modules to arrive at an overall total.

To find out the size unit you should use, measure the length of the house wall that adjoins your proposed patio site. If it's 24 feet long, six 4-foot rectangles will fit your wall dimensions exactly. If you plan to work with brick, tile, or rectangular concrete pavers, you should make your module an exact multiple of their dimensions (be sure to include space for any open joints).

The illustration below shows how an outdoor room can be designed using 5-foot-square modules. The L-shaped patio is made up of two sections that are 30 by 20 feet and 25 by 15 feet. The overhead, the path, the privacy trellis, the informal flagstone patio, and the raised flower bed all have dimensions that are multiples of 5 feet as well.

1 SQUARE = 5'

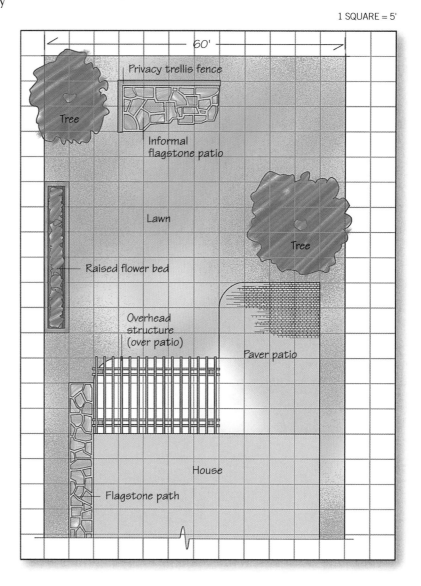

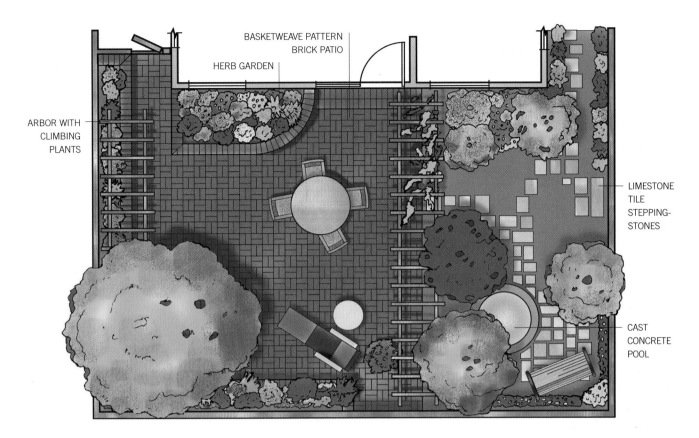

ARBOR WITH CLIMBING PLANTS

HERB GARDEN

BASKETWEAVE PATTERN BRICK PATIO

LIMESTONE TILE STEPPING-STONES

CAST CONCRETE POOL

THE PLAN VIEW DRAWING A plan view is a bird's-eye view of the patio layout. Draw it to scale and include as many details as possible. The plan view will give you a realistic idea of the available space and will help you estimate the quantity of materials that you need.

If you use a large enough piece of paper, you can even draw individual pavers to scale. Estimate the size of the stones to draw a flagstone patio plan view. To get a better idea of how the finished patio will look and how the space will feel,

sketch in accessories such as patio furniture and flowerpots.

DETAIL DRAWINGS Also make elevation, or side view, drawings. These should depict underlying structures as well as surface materials and show how things are put together. Be sure to detail the depth of the excavation, the thickness of the gravel and sand beds, and the length of any reinforcing materials. Also include any drainage solutions.

THE MATERIALS LIST As you draw, make an exhaustive list of all the materials you will need for the patio and any other structures you will build. If your list is accurate, it will save you extra trips to the supplier. You don't need to figure how many pavers or how much sand and gravel you will need, but you should indicate how many square feet will be covered; the masonry supplier can then calculate how much material you'll need.

BRICK PAVERS, 4" × 8" × 2½"

4 × 4 EDGING ANCHORED WITH ⅜" REBAR EVERY 4'

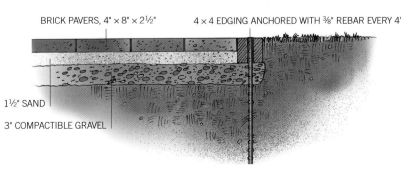

1½" SAND

3" COMPACTIBLE GRAVEL

gathering tools

Masonry tools are generally inexpensive, so you might as well spend a bit more for professional-quality tools. To achieve the best results, buy tools that feel comfortable in your hands and are made from metals that are precisely milled. Many better-quality tools are well coated or made of stainless steel, so they are less likely to rust than cheaper options.

In addition to the masonry hand tools shown here, you will probably need a basic set of carpentry tools, including a circular saw, drill, and hammer.

LAYOUT TOOLS The right tools enable you to quickly mark the perimeter of a patio. A carpenter's square lets you check small layouts for square. Mason's line makes accurate lines because it stays taut and does not stretch out. A chalk line lets you mark long, perfectly straight lines. You will also need a 25- or 30-foot tape measure as well as a 50- or 100-footer for large jobs. To check a layout or patio for level or correct slope, set a carpenter's level atop a long board or use a water level.

EXCAVATION TOOLS To remove sod and excavate a large area for a patio, consider renting a sod cutter or even a small earth-moving machine; see pages 137–39. To dig by hand, use a pointed shovel for basic digging and a square shovel to slice lines in the sod and to scrape the bottom of the excavated site. If you run into large roots or rocks, pry them up or cut them with a digging bar. Use a garden rake for smoothing excavated areas and for spreading gravel and sand. Drive stakes with a hand sledge.

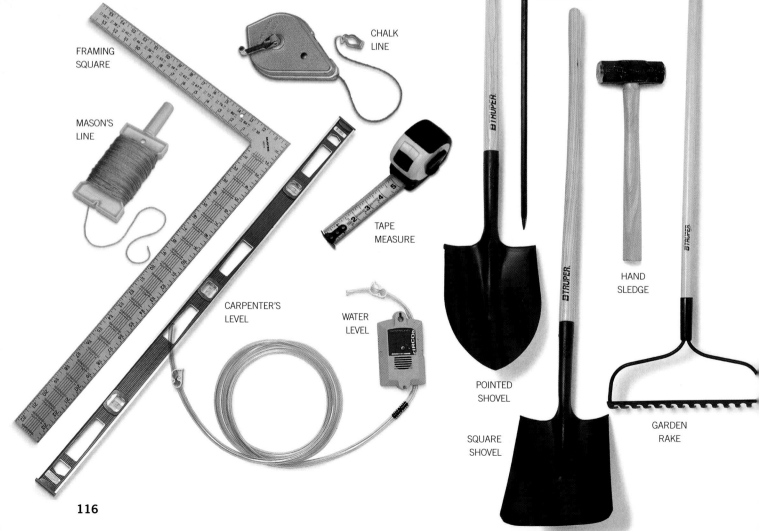

FRAMING SQUARE

MASON'S LINE

CHALK LINE

TAPE MEASURE

CARPENTER'S LEVEL

WATER LEVEL

DIGGING BAR

POINTED SHOVEL

SQUARE SHOVEL

HAND SLEDGE

GARDEN RAKE

TOOLS FOR CUTTING AND SETTING PAVERS For power tools that cut pavers easily and precisely, see pages 147–49. If you need to cut only a few pavers, use a brickset chisel to cut softer materials such as brick and a smaller-width cold chisel for harder materials. A mason's hammer lets you chip pavers roughly to shape as well as smooth cut edges. When tapping pavers into place, use a rubber mallet to prevent damaging them. Brick tongs will enable you to pick up and carry six or more bricks.

TOOLS FOR MORTAR AND CONCRETE Mix large batches of mortar in a wheelbarrow or mortar tub using a mason's hoe. Mix smaller batches in a bucket using a margin trowel. To spread mortar for tiles, use a notched trowel; use a pointed trowel if you need to slip mortar into joints. Finish a tile installation by spreading grout with a laminated grout float.

To smooth concrete you'll need special tools. If you will use the tools only once, consider renting rather than buying them. For the first round of finishing, use a bull float. For the second round, use a magnesium float. If you want a very smooth finish, a steel trowel is the right tool; however, it takes some practice to use correctly. Use an edger to round the edges of the slab and a concrete jointer to make control joints in the middle.

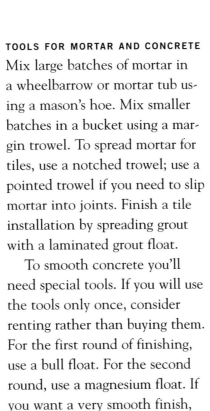

BRICKSET CHISEL

MASON'S HAMMER

COLD CHISEL

RUBBER MALLET

BRICK TONGS

MAGNESIUM FLOAT

EDGER

CONCRETE JOINER

NOTCHED TROWEL

MARGIN TROWEL

GROUT FLOAT

MASON'S HOE

BULL FLOAT

STEEL TROWEL

117

shopping for materials

A home center will probably carry a fair number of concrete pavers as well as small amounts of gravel or pebbles; you also may be able to order natural bricks and flagstones. For a full selection of paving materials—excluding tile—visit a dedicated masonry supply yard, sometimes called a stone yard or brickyard. There you will likely find both indoor displays and large outdoor bins containing paving materials in a wide variety of colors, sizes, shapes, and prices. A masonry supply source is also the best place for buying substrate materials, such as compactible gravel, mortar, and sand.

While masonry supply yards cater mostly to professional masons, their staff should be able to work with homeowners. If a salesperson does not give you the information you need, speak to another salesperson or go to another yard. You should feel free to wander around the yard and look at all the possibilities.

To buy flagstone, just figure the square footage you want to cover and have the salesperson roughly estimate the number of pounds (or tons) of material you will need. Poundage varies greatly depending on the thickness of the stones you choose. If you need only a small amount, you can carry it into the store and weigh it on a scale. For medium-sized loads that you can carry in your vehicle, the staff will weigh your van or truck when it's empty, then again after you load it with stone, and charge you for the difference. To buy a half ton or more, browse through the yard and choose a pallet or two full of stones for the yard to deliver.

Bricks and concrete pavers are sold by the unit rather than by weight, so your needs can be calculated more precisely.

Ask the staff detailed questions about delivery methods, and arrange for the delivery truck to drop heavy materials as close to your site as possible, without damaging your lawn or property. Keep these considerations in mind:

- If possible, have the gravel and/or sand dropped directly into the excavated site. If you need to have it unloaded on a nearby lawn, first spread thick-gauge plastic, then lay sheets of plywood for the materials to rest on. Make sure the material does not stay on the lawn for more than a few days or the grass may die.
- Be sure a load of pavers is not dropped onto your driveway. A 1-ton pallet of pavers can safely rest on a driveway as long as it is set down gently; if it is dropped from the truck (as often happens), the driveway will likely crack.
- If you need compactible gravel, sand, and pavers, plan the deliveries carefully. It is probably worthwhile to pay extra for two or even three separate deliveries if having all the materials delivered at once means that the pavers will end up inconveniently far from the site.

For a great range of tile choices, visit several tile stores.

working with professionals

A number of professionals can help with the design and construction of a patio. A landscape architect is trained and licensed to design and produce detailed plans for commercial and residential landscapes. Many landscape architects are willing to provide simple consultations for a fee. A landscape designer has less training, is probably not licensed, and is probably less expensive than an architect, but he or she may be more experienced working on residential projects.

A landscape contractor is trained to install all parts of a landscape, including patios, plants, walls, and irrigation systems. Some also offer design services. If you need only a patio or if you are comfortable planning and supervising construction, a subcontractor can save you money.

Whichever type of contractor you choose, be sure to check out the person's previous work by visiting patios he or she has installed and talking with former customers. A qualified contractor will gladly supply contact information for several customers.

Be sure to draw up a written contract for any work. The contract should stipulate:
- The plans to be followed as well as the materials to be used. List the exact types of pavers, edgings, and substrate materials as well as how they will be installed.
- Any penalties for work that is finished late.
- How any changes to the plan will be handled.
- Conditions that would result in suspension or termination of the contract.
- A payment plan that gives the contractor a fair amount of money up front for buying material but that withholds a substantial amount of money until all work is done to your satisfaction.

WORKING SAFELY

When cutting pavers, whether by hand or with a power saw, sharp chips are sure to fly around. Wear protective eyewear, gloves, a long-sleeved shirt, and long pants. When carting stones or other pavers, wear work boots preferably, with steel-reinforced toes, in case you drop a paver on your foot.

Masonry work stresses joints and muscles, especially those in the lower back, in unaccustomed ways. This can lead to serious, long-lasting back pain. But it is not only heavy lifting that can cause back strain. Repeatedly lifting and placing bricks and small pavers, especially if you are on your knees, may feel fine at the time but cause pain in the morning. The same holds true for digging with a shovel.

So take it easy, and don't be in a rush to finish the job. Stand up and stretch every few minutes and take plenty of breaks. Employ high school students for at least some of the grunt work. For a large excavation job, hire a company or rent a small earth-moving machine (see page 137). Lift with your legs, not your back: keep your back straight and bend your knees. A lifting belt can help prevent strain. If you need to carry very large stones, use a hand truck or work with a helper. If you do a lot of kneeling, knee pads will keep your knees from getting sore. If they're uncomfortable, use a kneeling pad instead.

quick and easy patios

The patios shown in this chapter do not demand any particular skills and can usually be laid in a day. They involve some heavy lifting but are simple to install because no edging is required. Thick, heavy flagstones and large concrete pavers are likely materials because they stay put. Patios made of these materials tend to have an informal look, with fairly wide joints between pavers.

flagstones set within sod

Rather than forming a distinct, clearly separate space, this patio blends with the lawn. To make it, select fairly flat, large stones. Small stones will be mostly covered when the grass grows tall. Larger stones—at least 12 inches across—are both more visible and more stable. The sod that you cut away for the stones can be used to patch brown spots elsewhere in the lawn.

You can also use this technique to create a stepping-stone path. Place the stones on the lawn and test that an adult can easily stride from stone to stone. Then cut the sod and set the stones in place.

1 Arrange the Stones

Place the stones on the lawn, moving them as needed to create a pleasing arrangement, and spacing them to create a path that's easy to walk on. If you will be placing furniture on the patio, see that chair and table legs will easily rest on the stones. With a sharp spade, cut the outline of all the stones in the sod. Remove each stone and dig out the sod to make a hole that conforms as closely as possible to the bottom of the stone.

2 Set the Stones

Place about half a shovelful of sand into each hole to help level and settle the stones. Replace the stones, setting them firmly into the sand. To ensure that the lawn mower can skim over the surfaces, make the top of each stone level with the surrounding lawn. When needed, add or remove sand to help make the stones level.

setting flagstones in soil

Flagstones can be set in sandlike bricks or concrete pavers (see pages 153–54) or mortared onto a concrete slab (see pages 168–71). But they also can be laid directly on tamped soil, as shown here. This method is slightly more elaborate than setting stones within sod (page 121); it works well for a larger patio area and also allows you to fill the joints with the crevice plants of your choice.

Choose flagstones that are fairly consistent in thickness; otherwise, it will be difficult to achieve an even surface. Flagstones are sold by the ton, so you can save plenty of money by buying thin stones that are about 1¼ inches thick.

1 Excavate the Site

A small amount of rainwater will soak into the joints between stones, but to prevent puddles from forming on the patio during a heavy rain, slope the excavation away from the house or to either side. Remove all sod (see page 138) and any roots larger than ½ inch in diameter. By scraping, rather than digging, the bottom of the excavation site, you'll keep undisturbed soil intact. Tamp the area with a hand tamper, 4-by-4 board, or power tamper, then gently rake to loosen a layer of soil about ½ inch thick. You may need to add some sand to make it easier to bed the stones.

2 Sort and Cut Stones

Have the stones delivered close to the site and set on sheets of plywood to protect the lawn. Sort the stones into three piles according to size. Choose stones from each pile as you lay the patio so that the various-sized stones will be evenly distributed.

Sandstone will cut easily while limestone will be tough to crack. If you have some very large stones, you may choose to keep them that way and space them regularly for dramatic effect. Or, you can score each stone with lines, break it apart, and lay the pieces with neat joints. See page 147 for cutting techniques.

3 Arrange the Stones

Place the stones in the excavated area and experiment with different arrangements. Aim to achieve joints that are fairly consistent in width, between ½ inch and 1 inch. This will take some time, so be patient. If a stone protrudes beyond the excavated area, you may choose to dig away the sod rather than cut the stone.

4 Bed the Stones

Once you have arranged about 10 square feet of stones, set them before moving on to the next section. To set a stone, stand on it or tap it with a rubber mallet to produce an impression in the soil. Tilt the stone up and use a garden trowel to scrape away soil or fill as needed. Lay the stone back down and test for stability. It may take several attempts before a stone is stable and level with its neighbors.

5 Fill the Joints

Once all the stones are firmly set, slip soil into the joints using a pointed shovel or a garden trowel. If you have chosen to embed crevice plants, do so now (see page 133). Because crevice soil gets tightly compacted, it is often best to add some sand to the potting mix to produce a soil that is firm but drains readily. Use soil that is slightly damp; soil that is too wet will be hard to clean and soil that is too dry will compress a great deal when it is moistened. Allow the soil to dry. Then gently sweep the stones until they are clean.

6 Spray, Plant, Seal

Set a hose nozzle to produce a fine mist and spray the patio until the joints are soaked. This will compress the soil. If you choose, sprinkle seeds into the joints. Wait for the soil to dry, add more soil as needed, and spray again. Allow the stones to dry, then gently sweep them clean. Unless the stones are very hard and nonporous, it is a good idea to paint them with a coating or two of acrylic sealer; this will give them a slightly wet look and make it much easier for you to keep them clean.

wood rounds or blocks

Though it may not last as long as stone, brick, or concrete pavers, wood can be a surprisingly long-lived paving material provided you choose the lumber carefully and install it correctly. Wood rounds and blocks are often installed with the grain facing up. That orientation enables moisture to soak in readily but also allows the wood to dry out quickly.

MATERIAL CHOICES

Choose wood that has proved durable in your area. Pressure-treated lumber rated "ground contact" is the most reliable and can last for decades as long as it dries out after rainfalls. The dark heartwood of redwood, cedar, or cypress will be almost as durable. To prolong the life of blocks or rounds, soak them in a sealer-preservative that contains an insecticide; consult with a local lumberyard to see what works in your area.

CUTTING ROUNDS

Wood rounds are not available at most lumberyards. If a neighbor or a municipal crew is cutting down a tree, it can be sliced into rounds using a chain saw. However, operating a chain saw can be dangerous, so approach this job with caution. Cut rounds will most likely have irregular thicknesses, which can make them difficult—but not impossible—to install. Leave the bark on the rounds if you like, but be aware that it may come apart and rot in a year or two.

This wood-round patio with wide joints makes for an interesting, rather than an easy, walking experience. Crevice plants will likely sink roots into the rounds as well as the soil.

CUTTING BLOCKS

If you have plenty of time or need only a few blocks, it's not difficult to cut 4 by 4s or 6 by 6s using a standard 7¼-inch circular saw. To cut a large number of blocks, use a power miter saw (also called a chop saw) or a radial-arm saw. A 10-inch saw will cut 4 by 4s, but you will need a 12-inch saw to cut through 6 by 6s or 4 by 6s.

Set up a simple jig like the one shown at right. Anchor the saw firmly, perhaps to a 2 by 12 resting on stable sawhorses. Place blocks on the 2 by 12 at the same height as the saw's base so you can easily rest a timber in place and slide it over after each cut. Fasten a stop block 3 inches or so from the blade so that each cut block will be exactly the same length.

The jig will allow you to cut factory style, but avoid working too quickly or you may burn out the blade—or, even worse, the saw. Give your equipment a rest when the saw starts to feel hot. If the cutting starts to go slowly, you probably need a new blade.

BUILDING A WOOD PATIO

Excavate the area to a depth that is 3 inches deeper than the thickness of the rounds or blocks. Add 2 inches of compactible gravel, tamp, and add 1 inch of sand.

Because wood rounds vary in shape, size, and thickness, you will need to experiment with different arrangements until you

By using a reliable chop saw and a simple jig, you can cut blocks with factory precision and speed. Here, the jig is made of two 2 by 4s attached to form an L shape that fits over the saw base.

create a pleasing pattern. Dig or add sand as needed to achieve a fairly even surface. Use a straightedge to check that the rounds are at the same height. Fill the gaps between rounds with gravel or pebbles mixed with sand for good drainage.

When setting wood blocks, use temporary plywood spacers to create ¼- or ½-inch joints; these will give the blocks some breathing space. Fill the joints with coarse sand or small-stoned gravel.

Wood rounds cut with a chain saw are rarely even in thickness, so expect to spend some time adjusting the substrate when you install them.

duckboards

Modular squares or rectangles made of decking material, often called duckboards, can be arranged and rearranged to suit your needs. Scatter them on a lawn to create an informal path or lay them close together to form a richly textured wood patio.

Manufactured duckboards (like those pictured above) are available in a variety of sizes, shapes, colors, and decking orientation. If your home center does not carry a good selection, type "modular decking" into a search engine to find several manufacturers. Most duckboards are made of long-lasting hardwood that is stained and finished and easily snapped together with plastic or stainless-steel clips. Duckboards made in a 45-degree pattern can be arranged in several ways.

To build your own duckboards, use rot-resistant lumber, especially for the sleepers (the underlying framing members). You may choose to use pressure-treated lumber rated "ground contact" for the sleepers and cedar or redwood for the decking boards.

If you want a duckboard to be square, you must cut the decking boards to a length that equals the width of a certain number of boards, including $\frac{1}{8}$-inch gaps between the boards. In our example, we cut 2 by 4s to $21\frac{5}{8}$ inches—the width of six 2 by 4s (6 times $3\frac{1}{2}$ inches, or 21 inches) plus five joints (5 times $\frac{1}{8}$ inch, or $\frac{5}{8}$ inch). Two other possible arrangements are nine 2 by 4s at $32\frac{1}{2}$ inches and five 2 by 6s (which are $5\frac{1}{2}$ inches wide) at 28 inches. Of course, if you choose joints wider than $\frac{1}{8}$ inch, the dimensions will change accordingly. It is possible that boards spanning more than 24 inches may be springy.

Hardwood duckboards can be quite moisture resistant as long as they are kept well protected with wood sealer. In this patio, some of the duckboards were cut with a jigsaw to follow the contours of the pool, then sealed to keep out water.

1 Make a Jig
Work on a flat surface. Cut four 2 by 4s to the desired length of the decking boards plus about 10 inches. Position the 2 by 4s into a square pattern as shown. See that the distance between boards in each direction is the same as the desired length of the decking boards and check all the corners for square. Drill pilot holes and drive two 2½-inch screws into each joint. Check again for square.

2 Cut the Decking and Sleepers
Set up a power saw with a jig so you can cut all the boards to the same length. Each duckboard in this design uses six 2-by-4 decking boards and two 2-by-3 sleepers.

3 Attach the Boards
Set the sleepers at both ends and place the decking boards on top. Use a nail as a spacer to maintain consistent joints between the decking boards. Drill pilot holes and drive two 2½-inch deck screws into each joint.

4 Set the Finished Duckboards
To prevent rot or mildew, place the duckboards on a flat area that has been excavated and filled with noncompactible gravel or pebbles for good drainage. You can lay duckboards on a concrete slab, but be sure to position them so that rainwater can easily drain underneath; all the sleepers should be parallel to the flow of water. If the area does not get very wet, position the sleepers perpendicular to the flow, first cutting several ½-inch notches in the boards to allow the water to run through.

In a heavily trafficked area, you may want to screw the duckboards together. Drill pilot holes and drive 2½-inch deck screws to tie two sleepers together.

informal circular patio

A small, detached brick circle like this makes a big visual impact yet can be built in a day and doesn't require much in the way of materials. Tuck it into a corner of your yard to create a peaceful private retreat.

For a patio that is 7 feet in diameter, you will need 134 standard-size bricks or concrete pavers plus a piece of slate or other decorative material for the central medallion. If you like, sprinkle the design with different colored or decorative bricks. Install bricks that are rated for use as pavers (see pages 100–103); if you live in a warm climate, you may choose to use wall bricks and perhaps protect them with a coat or two of acrylic sealer.

The photos here show how to install a patio on bare soil. If that is what you'll be doing, finish the installation by butting flexible invisible edging against the perimeter bricks and plant sod up against the edging. If the area is grassy, mark and cut your sod in a fairly precise circle and then butt the outside pavers against the grass.

1 Mark and Excavate

Place a stake in the center of the patio area. Tie a length of string to it and tie the other end to another stake; there should be 3½ feet of string between the two stakes. Trace the patio's outline with the second stake, marking it with lime, flour, or sand. Dig away any sod and roots. Dig deep enough to accommodate 3 inches of paver base (coarse sand mixed with small gravel, available at home centers and masonry yards) and the thickness of the bricks. Check the excavation for level using a level set atop a 2 by 4.

2 Pour and Tamp Sand

Pour three 1-cubic-foot bags of paver base into the excavated site and tamp firm using a hand tamper (as shown) or a 4 by 4. Check again for evenness and level and add or rake away paver base as needed. Spray with a fine mist from a hose and tamp again.

NUMBER OF BRICKS PER ROW

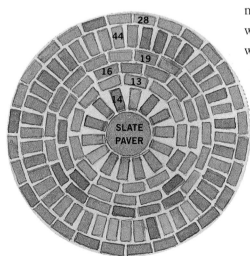

28
44
19
16
13
14
SLATE PAVER

3 Set the Pavers

Place the round paver in the exact middle of the sand circle. Working from the center outward, set down bricks in the pattern shown below. After placing each ring of bricks, stand back to inspect the arrangement and make adjustments as needed. To firmly bed the bricks, tap them with a rubber mallet; to ensure an even patio surface, use a 2-foot-long 2-by-4 beater board (see page 153). When you finish the outermost ring, you may choose to install flexible invisible edging or abut with sod.

4 Mortar the Center Paver and Fill Joints

Mix a one-bag batch of mortar (see page 167) adding colorant if desired. Using a brick trowel or a margin trowel, apply dabs of mortar under the center paver, then slip mortar between the bricks immediately surrounding it. Wipe away any excess with a clean, damp rag. Either allow the mortar to dry or work carefully when applying the joint sand, which is done by pouring sand over the entire patio and sweeping it into the joints. Spray the joints with a fine mist, allow to dry, then repeat the process.

paving with concrete chunks

This paving material is one that you can likely get for free; in fact, a neighbor may even pay you to haul it away. One person's junk is another's treasure, and concrete chunks have become a popular paving material in recent years. As long as it is not stained, old concrete has a pebbly charm, and you can feel good both about saving money and making an environmentally friendly choice.

To evaluate a concrete slab for stability, see page 76. If your old concrete slab is ugly but solid, you can stain it, paint it, or pave over it with brick, concrete pavers, flagstone, tile, or even pebbles (see pages 78–81 and 168–79). If the slab is falling apart, you may just want to get rid of it; if you prefer a patio with plant-filled joints rather than a solid slab, it's time to get out the old sledgehammer.

DEMOLISHING CONCRETE

Many patio and sidewalk slabs are only 2 to 3 inches thick and have no metal reinforcing, making them surprisingly easy to break apart and haul away. While a well-built patio may be 4 inches thick and a driveway thicker still, a motivated homeowner can most likely handle the demolition.

Because a lot of heavy labor is involved, start in an out-of-the-way corner to gauge the difficulty. You can always call in pros if the task proves too hard.

To cut the concrete into certain shapes, first use a circular

Pieces of broken concrete are put to good use as pavers for a pathway. As with most paving materials, crevice plants enhance the appearance.

saw equipped with a masonry blade to cut ½-inch-deep lines; the concrete will usually crack along those lines if you hammer carefully. For precise shapes, pound with a small sledge and a chisel. Wear long pants and a long-sleeved shirt, gloves, a dust mask, and eye protection; sharp chips sometimes fly around.

First, try whacking the slab with a sledgehammer; it may break apart. If not, insert a wrecking bar, which is about 6 feet long, under the slab; you may have to dig an insertion point for the bar. Place a stone or a scrap of lumber under the bar to act as a fulcrum, then pry up the concrete. Have a helper hold the concrete up while you beat it with a sledge. Once the

concrete is raised above the ground, you can break it apart with relative ease.

If the slab is reinforced with wire mesh, cut the wire with lineman's pliers or wire cutters. The wire ends are sharp and rusty, so work carefully. If you encounter ⅜- or ½-inch rebar, you'll need a pair of bolt cutters.

MAKING A USED-CONCRETE PATIO

If the new patio will be in the same location as the current slab, you can crack the old slab and spread out the pieces to create fairly consistent joints. If the new patio will be in another spot, you may want to number the chunks so you can reassemble them in the same order. Set the chunks

on tamped soil or lay them on a sand bed. Concrete is thick, so you will need to excavate the ground fairly deep.

Follow the procedure on pages 122–23 to firmly bed and level the chunks. You may choose to acid-clean, acid-stain, or paint them. Sow seeds or insert crevice plants in the joints.

ANOTHER USE FOR OLD CONCRETE

The broken edge of a concrete chunk reveals an attractive pattern of cemented pebbles of various sizes and colors, making concrete chunks a good choice for a flower bed or a low wall. Because the chunks are fairly consistent in thickness, you can stack them easily.

english-style construction

The following method of constructing a patio—setting pavers in dabs of mortar atop a tamped gravel and sand base—is commonly used by our friends "across the pond," where winters are freezing but not severe. The technique is not suitable for patios composed of bricks or small concrete pavers, but works well with cut stones, flagstones, large concrete pavers, or large, heavy tiles.

The English method holds pavers more securely than those set in sand, so you do not need edging. The resulting patio is not quite as firm as one set in a mortar base atop a concrete slab (see pages 168–71), but installation is much easier if you do not already have a slab in place. This construction method also lets you put plants in the joints.

Setting pavers in mortar dabs is a good technique to use when pavers are not uniform in thickness. You can simply push down harder to set a paver lower or add more mortar if you need to set one higher.

The project shown here is an informal patio with fairly wide plant-filled joints and ragged edges. The stones are second-quality bluestone, meaning they vary in color and often have one uncut edge. This makes them less expensive than precisely cut bluestone of a uniform color—and more interesting to look at.

1 Arrange and Cut the Stones
Dig up the sod where the patio will be and excavate to a depth about 3 inches deeper than the

lawn. Using pieces of scrap 1-by lumber as spacers, set the pavers in a dry run. Stretch guidelines to maintain straight joints and experiment with different arrangements to create attractively offset joints. You may choose to have all the joints uniform in width—in which case you will need to cut a good number of pavers—or you may decide to permit occasional variation in joint width and shape for a more casual look.

To produce a ragged edge, allow some of the pavers to lap onto the lawn. Once you have settled on a pattern that pleases you, cut around the overlapping stones with a square shovel, as shown on page 121. Remove the pavers, number them on the back with a crayon, and stack them in the correct orientation so you can replace them exactly.

2 Screed with Gravel and Sand

Tamp the soil with a hand tamper, a piece of 4 by 4, or a vibrating power tamper. Spread 2 inches of compactible gravel in the excavated area and use a length of 1 by 4 or 2 by 4 to screed it evenly. Tamp the gravel, then add and screed a 1-inch layer of rough sand. Alternatively, screed and tamp 3 inches of paver base (see page 129).

3 Add Five Dabs of Mortar

Set seven or eight pavers in place, reinsert the 1-by spacers,

and make sure you've got the pavers all facing the right way. Mix a batch of mortar (see page 167). Pick up the paver that is highest and plop five dabs of mortar on the area beneath it. If the paver is not close to square in shape, you may use four or six dabs; the important thing is to get a fairly even distribution of mortar.

4 Bed the Pavers

Press several pavers into dabs of mortar, then use a straight board to press them firmly into the mortar and create an even surface. If a paver is too high, use a mallet or a hammer and a board to press it down. If one is too low, pick it up, add more mortar, and replace it. Lay all the pavers this way. If mortar oozes out the sides, scrape most of it away. Keep a few damp rags handy to wipe away any mortar smears as soon as they appear.

5 Plant the Joints

Wait a day or two for the mortar to set. To make pavers easy to clean and resist staining, you may choose to paint them with a coat or two of acrylic sealer. Now you're ready for the finishing touch: partially fill the joints with soil that is suited to the crevice plants you have chosen. Sow seeds and cover with soil or break apart plants and insert them, as shown.

dry-laid patios with edging

By setting bricks or concrete pavers in a bed of firmly tamped gravel and sand, you create a surface that is rock-solid and sure to last many years. The patios in this chapter are a bit more difficult to build than those in the previous chapter, but they are well within the reach of a motivated homeowner. No special skills are required, but you will need to proceed systematically; we'll show you how.

laying out the patio

Once you have determined the outline of your patio (see pages 112–15), you should take the time to mark the perimeter precisely. The outline should take into account the width of the edging as well as any stakes that are used to hold the edging in place.

A patio can be laid out quickly using lines attached to stakes, but batterboards make better guides and take only a small amount of time to build and use. Batterboards are not easily bumped out of position and make it easy for you to adjust or remove and replace guidelines as needed.

Make a batterboard like the one shown at right by attaching a 2-foot-long 1 by 4 to two 1-by-2 stakes. Make the stakes about 18 inches long—longer if the ground is very soft and shorter if it is very hard.

The illustration below gives an overview of the layout process. Estimate the outline of the patio, then pound two batterboards into the ground about 2 feet beyond the estimated location of each corner, one on each side of the corner. If the patio will have a rounded edge,

position the batterboards 2 feet beyond where straight lines would intersect. Stretch strings to indicate the patio outline.

BATTERBOARD

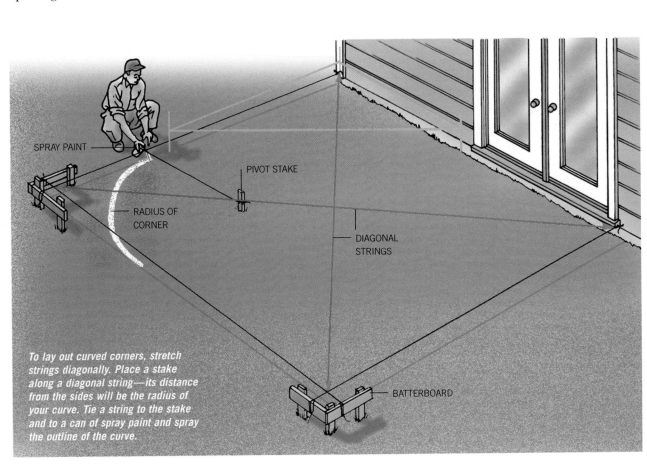

SPRAY PAINT

PIVOT STAKE

RADIUS OF CORNER

DIAGONAL STRINGS

BATTERBOARD

To lay out curved corners, stretch strings diagonally. Place a stake along a diagonal string—its distance from the sides will be the radius of your curve. Tie a string to the stake and to a can of spray paint and spray the outline of the curve.

CHECKING FOR SQUARE

It's important that a rectangular patio have square corners; otherwise, you will end up making lots of extra cuts and the patio will look unprofessional. If you are installing wood or invisible edging, remove sod to accommodate the wood stakes or the back flange of the invisible edging.

1 Run the Lines

Drive a nail or screw or pound a single stake against the house to indicate the perimeter of the patio. Do the same to indicate the line where sod must be removed.

Tightly stretch mason's line from the house to the batterboard on both sides of the patio. The strings should be close to the ground but not touch the grass at any point. Temporarily wrap the lines around the batterboard so that you can easily shift their positions. For the line that is parallel to the house, measure to position both ends the same distance from the house.

2 Measure for Square

To check a corner for square, mark a spot on the house precisely 6 feet from the corner. Use a piece of tape to mark the adjacent string exactly 8 feet from the corner. If the distance between the two marks is precisely 10 feet, then the corner is square. If not, move the string as needed. If the patio is large, then use multiples of 3, 4, and 5 (such as 12, 16, and 20 or 30, 40, and 50). Check

the other corners using the same method.

Double-check for square by measuring the diagonals, which should be the same length. When you are certain of the lines' positions, nail or screw them in place on the batterboards. Then mark the batterboards so you can

remove and correctly replace the lines during the construction process.

3 Mark a Corner

To mark a corner, use the lines attached to the batterboards, which you established close to the ground as guides for excavation; if the lines are high, they could be difficult to use. First, find the exact location of a corner: dangle a chalk line (or a plumb bob) so that its string nearly touches the intersection of the two guidelines and the weight nearly rests on the ground. Drive a stake into the ground or dig out some sod to mark the exact corner. Then drive stakes and stretch lines to use as guides for excavating.

4 Mark for a Curve

To create a radius curve (that is, a portion of a circle), make a compass as shown on page 135. Drive a stake at a point along a diagonal line between two corners. Tie a mason's line to the stake, wrap the other end around a can of paint, and spray a line. Make the curve tighter or more sweeping by moving the stake closer to or farther away from the corner.

To create a curve that is not a simple radius, lay a garden hose on the ground in the desired shape. Pour sand, flour, or lime over the hose all along its length. When you pick up the hose, a clear outline will be revealed.

excavating for a patio

The instructions on the next three pages show how to remove sod, excavate to the correct depth, and lay and power-tamp 3 to 6 inches of compactible gravel.

However, depending on your soil conditions and climate, you may not need this depth of gravel and may be able to simply tamp the soil firm and screed an inch or two of sand on top (see page 150). Check with a pro or with your building department to find out how thick the gravel and sand layers should be in order to solidly support a patio in your area.

If the patio will be rained on a lot, or if it is larger than 500 square feet, you may need to provide drainage; see pages 108–9.

Before you start digging, plan where to place the excavated sod and soil. You may be able to use one or both somewhere in your yard. If not, advertise in a local paper; someone may be happy to haul it all away.

THE ORDER OF WORK
Carefully think through your patio installation step by step. Often, the best sequence is: (1) remove sod and all organic material (see page 138, top); (2) install edgings at the finished height of the patio (pages 140–46); and (3) string a grid of guidelines across the edgings and excavate to the correct depth (pages 138–39).

However, if you will be installing a decorative edging that is uneven or an invisible edging, first remove the sod, then cut and stake temporary 2-by-4 guides at the patio height and use them to measure for the depth of excavation.

To minimize the need to cut patio pavers, hold off on the edging for one or two sides. Temporarily install 2 by 4s as a height

guide for those sides. Once you have laid all or most of the pavers, install the final section of the edging snug against the last row of pavers (see page 153).

PLANNING FOR THE RIGHT DEPTH
In most cases, it is best to install a patio just slightly above grade so you can run a lawn mower over it. If the yard is uneven, you may need to fill in low spots; you can use the soil and sod that were removed during excavation. Some edgings require a trench that is deeper than the rest of the excavation.

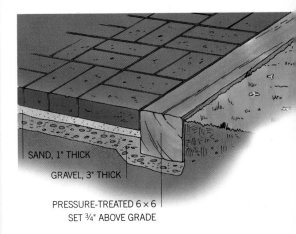

SAND, 1" THICK

GRAVEL, 3" THICK

PRESSURE-TREATED 6 × 6 SET ¾" ABOVE GRADE

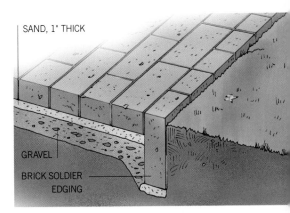

SAND, 1" THICK

GRAVEL

BRICK SOLDIER EDGING

REMOVING SOD

For a small patio, dig up sod with a square shovel. Cut a line around the perimeter holding the shovel blade vertically. Slice a parallel line about 18 inches inside the first line. Undercut the sod between the two lines while a helper rolls it up.

For a larger area, rent a power sod cutter (below), which greatly eases the task. Power cutters also cut straight lines, producing more usable rolls of sod.

With the sod stripped away, dig and remove any other organic matter, including roots thicker than 1/2 inch.

MEASURING FOR LEVEL OR THE CORRECT SLOPE

If your edging requires that you remove sod in an area greater than the size of the patio, move the guidelines over to indicate the perimeter of the edging. At each corner, pound a stake firmly into the ground directly below the string lines. Stretch mason's line between the stakes to indicate both the perimeter and the height of the edging.

To drain well, a patio should slope down and away from the house at least 1/4 inch per foot; where it is parallel to the house, the patio should be level. Along your house, mark a level refer-ence line to indicate the finished height of the patio—about 1 inch below the bottom of the door threshold.

First, mark the corner stake for level. If the patio is 16 feet wide or less, check for level with a carpenter's level on a long, straight board (see below). To measure a longer distance, use a water level. Then measure down at least 1/4 inch per foot and attach the string line at that point (inset). (To follow the contours of the lawn, you may want to install the patio at a greater slope.) The line and the stake may get bumped, so check them from time to time.

EXCAVATING TO THE RIGHT DEPTH

Install either the finished edging (see pages 140–46) or temporary 2-by-4 guides staked at the finished height of the patio (page 182). You will use the edging as a guide for the depth of the excavation, so attach it firmly and check it from time to time to make sure it has not been bumped out of position.

If possible, a patio substrate should rest on undisturbed soil that has never been dug up. Aim to excavate to the exact required depth and no deeper.

To calculate how deep to dig, add the thickness of the gravel, the sand, and the pavers. A typical installation calls for 3 to 4 inches of compacted gravel and 1 inch of sand.

Stretch a grid of mason's line across the edging, spacing the lines 4 to 5 feet apart in both directions. If the edging is wood, simply drive nails or screws and tie the lines to them. If the edging is brick, tie the lines to stakes driven a foot or two outside the patio perimeter, so that the lines rest on top of the bricks. Pull the lines very taut.

Your shovel blade may be the correct length to use as a depth guide. If not, mark the depth with a piece of tape on the blade or handle. That way, you can quickly check for depth as you work. Dig first with a pointed shovel, then use a square shovel to scrape the bottom.

ADDING GRAVEL AND TAMPING

Order compactible gravel (also known as aggregate base course or hardcore) made to serve as a patio substrate. To figure how much you need in cubic yards, see page 180. If possible, have the supplier dump the gravel directly into the excavated area. Otherwise, you will need to use a wheelbarrow.

Remove the guidelines. An hour or two before the gravel will be delivered, rent a vibrating plate compactor to power-tamp first the soil and then the gravel. You may also want to rent a vibrating plate compactor to tamp the finished paver surface (see page 154).

Spread the gravel with a shovel, then rake it. Reinstall the guidelines and check for depth; note that tamping will likely lower the depth by about $\frac{1}{2}$ inch. Remove the lines, power-tamp several times, and recheck the depth.

lumber edging

Cut stakes from pressure-treated 2 by 4s or 1 by 4s if the ground is firm. The stake length depends on soil conditions; it should take some effort to drive them. Use a 2-by-4 scrap, as shown below, to prevent splitting the stakes as you drive them about 1½ inches below the top of the edging. If the soil is hard and wood stakes tend to move the edging out of position, metal stakes may be the solution.

Check again that the edging is correctly aligned. From inside the excavation, drive two 2½-inch deck screws into each stake. Shovel gravel under the edging to support it at all points. Backfill with soil and lightly tamp with a 2 by 4. After the patio is laid, tamp the soil firm.

Edging made with 2-by lumber or bender board adds a subtle distinction; for a more dramatic effect, use timbers (see page 142). Pressure-treated lumber rated "ground contact" is durable and inexpensive. The dark heartwood of redwood is better looking but is expensive and not as resistant to rot. Light-colored redwood or cedar will likely rot within a few years. Plastic or composite decking is completely resistant to rot and can be bent into gentle curves.

STRAIGHT RUNS

Select 2-by-4 or 2-by-6 boards that are straight and free of large knots. If possible, buy long boards so you can avoid butt joints. If you cut a board, apply a generous coat or two of sealer to the cut end.

The edging must be supported with stakes approximately every 2 feet. Cut the sod back 2 inches from the outside of the edging to make room for the stakes. Excavate deep enough to place 2 to 3 inches of noncompactible gravel under the boards.

Cut the boards to length and set them in place, resting both ends on gravel. Use a level or guidelines to see that the boards are at the right height and are either level or correctly sloped. Sight along each board to see that it is straight. Check the edging for square (see page 136).

TURNING CURVES

For the sake of appearance, you may want curved edging to be the same thickness as any 2-by edging it abuts. For gentle curves, you may be able to use 1 by 4s. Soaking a 1 by 4 in water overnight will make it more flexible. To make tight bends you can use redwood bender board, about ⅜ inch thick, but it is difficult to find in some areas. A lumberyard may rip-cut bender board pieces out of 2 by 4s for a modest price. Plastic or composite decking boards are fairly bendable and may be close enough in color to wood.

Because you cannot accurately measure the length of a curve, install pieces that are longer than you need and cut them to length after they are fully installed.

1 Use Stakes to Make the Curve

Drive stakes, 1½ inches below the top of the edging, at the beginning and end of the curved run, on the outside of the patio. Bend the edging board to the desired shape and drive temporary stakes on the inside to hold it in place. Stand back and examine the curve. You may need to remove and reinstall a stake or two in order to achieve a smooth curve.

2 Attach Permanent Stakes

Check that the edging is level or correctly sloped. Every 2 feet or so, drive a permanent stake on the outside so that its top is 1½ inches below the top of the edging. Drill pilot holes and drive deck screws to attach the bender boards to the permanent stakes. Remove the temporary stakes.

3 Cut the Ends

At the point where the curve ends and a straight line begins, use a small square to draw a cut-off line. Cut the curved edging at the line with a handsaw or a reciprocating saw. When you install the abutting straight edging piece, drive a stake that attaches to both the curved and the straight edging; this will ensure a smooth transition.

timber edging

Large timbers impart a rough-hewn look to your patio. If you are lucky you can find railroad ties or other massive, weather-beaten pieces. However, pressure-treated 4-by-6 or 6-by-6 lumber is a fine alternative; it will crack nicely and turn a rustic gray in a year or two. Be sure the lumber is rated for ground contact. As much as possible, select timbers that are straight; there is no way to unbend them. Excavate deep enough to accommodate several inches of gravel under the timbers.

Rustic timbers serve as retaining walls on this patio, keeping gravel in place and out of bordering plant beds.

CUTTING AND POSITIONING

To cut a 4 by 6, use a small square to draw lines around all four sides. Set the blade of a 7½-inch circular saw to full depth and check that the blade is square to the saw's base. Cut the two opposite sides of the 4 by 6. Cut a 6 by 6 on all four sides, then cut the middle with a handsaw or a reciprocating saw.

Set the timbers in a bed of gravel and check for correct height and alignment. You may need to remove the timber, add or shovel away some gravel, and try again. Check the edging for square (see page 136).

ANCHORING

Secure the timbers with either ½-inch concrete reinforcing bar ("rebar") or ½-inch galvanized pipe; either will rust attractively in a year or so. Equip a drill with an extra long spade bit as wide as the anchors you will use. Drill holes through the center of the timber every 2 feet or so. If your drill or bit starts to get hot, give the drill a rest.

Use a hacksaw or a reciprocating saw equipped with a metal-cutting blade to cut a 3-foot length of rebar or pipe. Use a small sledge to pound an anchor through the drilled hole until its top is flush with the timber. If the pounding is difficult, cut the remaining anchors shorter; if it is easy, cut them longer.

invisible edging

Once backfilled, this type of edging can be completely covered. When you excavate for the patio, allow room for the edging's outer flange. In most cases, it is installed after the excavation is completed and the gravel—but not the sand—is laid. See pages 152–53 for how to lay and screed sand for this type of installation.

GETTING THE RIGHT POSITION

Because the edging will rest on top of the gravel, take care that the gravel is even and at least close to the correct height. To inhibit the growth of unwanted weeds, you may choose to lay landscaping fabric over the gravel before installing the edging (see page 150).

Set the edging in place and check for square (see page 136). The edging height does not have to be precise, but it should not be more than ½ inch too high or

Invisible edging bends easily to fit curves and angles, making it an ideal choice for rounded patios. Here, it virtually disappears between the small stone sitting area and lawn.

too low. You may need to add or remove gravel to maintain the correct height.

ANCHORING WITH SPIKES

Along straight runs, drive stakes through the edging's holes every

foot or so, more often if the ground is soft and the spikes are easy to drive. At a curve, drive a spike into every available hole.

Once the patio is laid, fill in behind the edging with strips of excavated sod.

paver edging

This type of edging typically consists of the same bricks or concrete pavers that make up the rest of the patio, but you may prefer to use a contrasting material. These pages show how to lay the pavers in sand and soil, which will produce a firm edging if your soil and sod are stable. For extra stability, back the pavers with invisible edging (see page 143). Or, set the soldiers—pavers that stand upright with their edges, not their faces, facing the patio—in several inches of mortar. (Sailor pavers stand upright with their faces toward the patio, an arrangement that takes fewer pavers but is weaker than a soldier edging.) If you prefer to lay the edging pavers flat rather than on end, set them in concrete (see page 145).

Installing paver edging is easier if you cut a straight line in the sod and snug the pavers against the sod. You may need to tamp soil between the pavers and the sod in some places.

1 Trench, Then Screed Sand

Stretch a guideline at the level of the patio surface. Then dig a trench 4 inches deeper than the height of the pavers. Shovel in 3 inches of compactible gravel or paver base and tamp firm with a hand tamper or a piece of 4 by 4. Make a screed guide as shown from a 2 by 6 and a 2 by 4; the 2 by 6 should extend below the 2 by 4 by the length of a soldier. Pour damp sand over the gravel. Scrape across the sand with the guide; the 2 by 4 should be just barely above the line. Spray the

sand with a fine mist of water, then add a little more sand and screed one more time.

2 Bed the Pavers

Position each paver so that its outside corner is about $1/8$ inch from the guideline. Set about 4 feet of pavers, then lay a straight board on top and tap it to achieve a smooth, even surface.

3 Tamp Firm

Use a 2 by 4 to gently tamp soil on the patio side. If the pavers move out of alignment and need to be nudged back toward the patio side, use the edge of a piece of plywood to tamp the soil into the space that lies between the sod and the soldiers. If the pavers won't stay put, temporarily stake a 2 by 4 to their outside edge.

TURNING A CURVE

To set edgings in a smooth curve, install bender board edging supported with stakes (see page 141). The joints between the pavers will be wider on the outside of the curve.

SETTING AN EDGING IN MORTAR OR CONCRETE

To set pavers in mortar, first pour a concrete edging, as shown on page 146. Make the top lower than the patio by the thickness of the pavers you will install. Set the pavers in troweled mortar, as described on pages 178–79, using a straightedge or a guideline to align them. Leave ⅜-inch-wide joints between the pavers and fill them with mortar, or set the pavers snug against each other and sweep sand into the joints.

To set pavers in wet concrete (as shown at right), build a form for concrete edging (see page 146), but use 2 by 6s instead of 2 by 4s. The form should be just wide enough to accommodate the pavers. Make a screed guide that extends below the top of the forms by the thickness of the pavers you will install minus ½ inch (the pavers will sink ½ inch into the concrete).

Pour a bag of concrete mix into a wheelbarrow or large trough and add two shovels of Portland cement for greater strength. Mix with water and pour into the form. Use the screed guide to level the con-

crete. Immediately set pavers in the wet concrete using spacers to keep them ⅜ inch apart. Gently tap each paver so that it settles flush with the top of the form

boards; you may need to raise or lower the concrete to accomplish this. After the concrete has hardened, fill the joints with mortar (see page 179).

concrete edging

This method produces a solid edging and is not that difficult to install. To avoid an industrial look, you can tint the concrete while it is wet or give it a decorative finish when it is poured (see pages 187–88). Or, you can wait for the concrete to cure and then stain it or cover it with tile, flagstone, or pavers.

For general instructions on building forms and mixing and finishing concrete, see pages 180–86. Use fiberglass-reinforced concrete or cut pieces of wire reinforcing mesh to fit into the forms before you pour the concrete. The edging should be at least 6 inches wide and 4 inches deep; anything less massive is likely to crack. If you plan to cover the edging with tiles or pavers, make the edging an appropriate width.

Begin by digging a trench wide enough to accommodate the edging plus the thickness of the framing boards. Spread 3 inches of compactible gravel at the bottom and use a 2 by 4 or 4 by 4 to tamp it firm. Build straight forms using 2 by 4s held in place with 1-by-2 or 2-by-2 stakes; use bender board for any curved edges. Check that the forms are at the right height and either level or correctly sloped.

See page 180 to learn how to calculate your concrete needs. Mix batches of concrete in a wheelbarrow if you need less than ½ yard; order concrete delivered in a truck if you need more. Pour or shovel the concrete into the forms. Poke all along the forms with a piece of 1 by 2 or rebar to minimize air bubbles. Screed the top with a scrap of lumber that you work with a sawing motion.

Use a magnesium float to further smooth the top and an edging tool to smooth the edges. Once the concrete has started to harden, remove the forms. If the outside edge will be exposed, float it as well. For a finished appearance, work the surface with a steel trowel or brush it lightly with a broom. Cover the concrete with plastic and/or spray it regularly for the next four days so that it can cure slowly.

TILE EDGING

To set tiles on a concrete edging, mix and spread latex-reinforced thin-set mortar using a square-notched trowel. Set the tiles in the mortar and use plastic spacers to maintain consistent grout joints. Wait overnight for the mortar to harden, then fill the joints with grout (see page 174).

cutting pavers

For many patios, bricks and concrete pavers need to be cut precisely to fit snugly against the edging or the house. Even a few poorly cut pavers can make a patio look sloppy, so take the time and use the proper tools to do it right. If you have only 20 or so cuts to make, you may choose to cut by hand with a chisel. For more cuts, rent a brick splitter or a masonry saw.

MARKING FOR CUTS

Install all the full-sized pavers, then measure for cutting the end pieces. This streamlines the cutting process and reduces the time needed to use a rental saw.

Rather than measuring, you will usually get a tighter fit if you hold the paver in place and mark it for a cut. If the cut is angled, mark for both sides of the cut, then draw a straight line between the marks. To ensure that you are getting the right angle, use a T-bevel (see top right). Hold it in place, then tighten the nut to preserve the angle.

CUTTING BY HAND

While some types of flagstone and brick break apart with just a tap or two, others call for a more concerted effort. Most concrete pavers are simply too hard to cut by hand.

CUTTING FLAGSTONE is an unpredictable process; don't be surprised if a cut fails to follow the line you had in mind. For best results, use a brickset or narrow cold chisel to score a line on both sides of the stone. Position the stone with the scored line on top of a pipe or a scrap of wood. Using a small sledge, hit the stone on the waste side to break it off.

TO CUT A BRICK OR CONCRETE PAVER, place it on a flat, resilient surface, such as a bed of sand. Press a brickset chisel firmly in place and tap with a hammer to score a line on all four sides. Hold the brickset against a score line with its bevel (the angled side of the tip) facing the waste side of the cut. Whack the brickset hard to break the brick. Chip or scrape away any protrusions along the cut edge with a brick trowel or the chisel. If the break occurs in the wrong place, throw the brick out and try another.

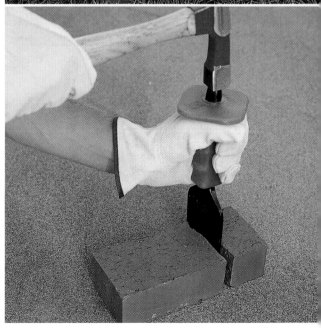

USING A BRICK SPLITTER

A brick splitter can be rented for a modest price. It makes fairly accurate cuts quickly, but edges will be a bit ragged. Mark the cut line and align it with the splitter's blade. Or, use the splitter's ruler to measure for the cut. Make sure that the brick is pressed firmly against the guide. Push down forcefully on the handle to break the brick.

USING A CIRCULAR SAW

You can make precise, clean cuts using a circular saw equipped with a masonry-cutting blade or a diamond blade. Be aware that the dust created by cutting masonry can eventually damage a circular saw, especially an inexpensive model; use this technique only if you have a professional-grade saw or if you need to cut only 20 or so pavers. If the saw begins to heat up, be sure to take a break to allow the motor to cool.

Attach a scrap piece of wood to the working surface to keep the bricks from sliding as you cut. Clamp several bricks together as shown below to cut them all to the same length. Set the blade to a depth of about ¾ inch; if the cutting is difficult, reduce the depth of the cut. Press the saw firmly down on the pavers as you make the cut. Lower the blade and make a second pass, and repeat until you have cut most of the way through. Then break off the waste with a hammer and chisel or, for greater precision, finish the cut from the other side.

Brick splitter

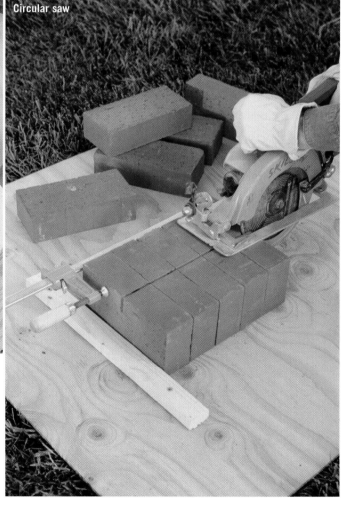

Circular saw

USING A WET SAW

A wet-cutting masonry saw, also called a tub saw, is the best tool for making numerous clean, accurate cuts on pavers of all sorts as well as on tiles. Buying a wet saw will save you the hassle of running to the rental store every time you want to cut masonry or tile, but an inexpensive saw will cut more slowly and may not be as accurate as a rental saw; its blade also may not be deep enough to cut a concrete paver and may become dull after making 30 or so cuts.

If you rent, be sure to get complete operating instructions. Test that the tray glides smoothly and is square to the blade. Also check that you have all the guides you need for making angle cuts.

BASIC OPERATION When using this tool, water must spray onto the blade constantly; even a few seconds of dry cutting can dull a blade. If the unit you're using places the pump in a 5-gallon bucket filled with water, refill the bucket when it runs out of water by opening a drain hole in the pan of the saw. If the pump is placed in the pan, there is rarely a need to refill. However, the blade will last longer if you regularly throw out dirty water and replace it with clean.

To make a basic cut, place the paver in the tray and hold it against the back guide so it is square to the blade. Turn on the saw and check that water flows to the blade. Slide the tray forward slowly to slice through the paver.

ANGLE CUT Typical guides hold a paver at 45 degrees and other specified angles; an adjustable angle guide is also available. You can also use a small square, as shown. Hold the paver firmly against the guide as you slide the tray forward to make the cut.

NOTCH CUT Make two cuts for a notch (or cutout). Tilt the paver up to avoid overcutting the top of the paver; the bottom of the cut should be slightly longer than the top. Hold the paver against the back guide to ensure a square cut.

CURVE CUT This cut takes time to make. Hold the paver firmly with both hands and tilt it up so that the bottom of the cut will be slightly deeper than the top. Press the paver gently against the blade and move it from side to side to gradually shave the paver to the desired shape.

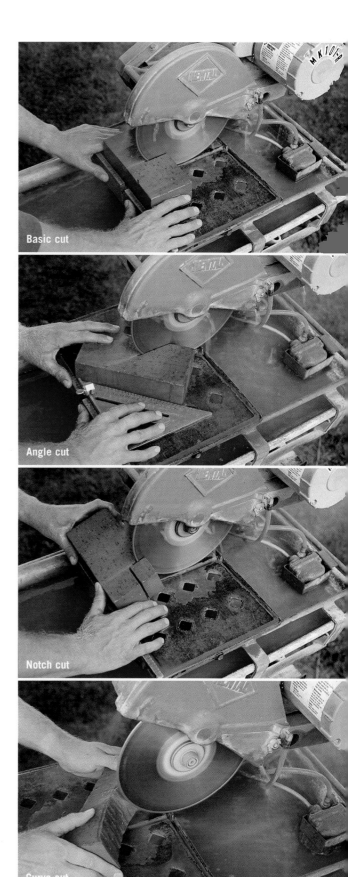

Basic cut

Angle cut

Notch cut

Curve cut

screeding a solid-edged patio

Once the site has been excavated, the edging has been installed, and gravel has been spread and tamped (see pages 137–46), you can use the edging as a guide to spread and screed the sand on which the pavers will rest. If you plan to use invisible edging or edging that is not at the same height as the patio surface, follow the pipe screeding technique that is shown on page 152.

Local codes may specify using 1 or 2 inches of sand. Measure down from the grid lines (see page 138) in a number of places to check the average depth; power-tamping may have compacted the gravel, so you may need a little more sand than you originally planned. The pavers should end up about ¼ inch above the edging; this makes it easier to sweep the patio clean of debris.

Use coarse sand, sometimes called torpedo sand, for the underlayment; later, you will need fine sand or stone dust to fill the joints between pavers.

1 Lay Fabric

Check with local contractors or your building department to see if landscaping fabric is needed in your area. If so, roll heavy-duty landscaping fabric over the gravel base. Work carefully to eliminate folds. Cut the pieces accurately and butt them tightly against the edging, where weeds may grow. Overlap parallel strips by 6 to 8 inches. Hold the sheets in place with mounds of sand.

2 Install a Temporary Screed Guide

If the patio is less than 10 feet wide, skip this step. For a larger patio, cut a 2 by 4 to fit and attach it 6 to 10 feet away from, and parallel to, one side of the edging. Attach it at the same height as the edging. Screw the 2 by 4 to the edging or to the house at both ends. Every 3 or 4 feet, drive a 2-by-4 stake against the temporary screed guide outside the area to be screeded (see Step 4) and about an inch below the top of the 2 by 4. Double-check the guide's height all along its length.

3 Build a Screed

Make the screed from a 2 by 4 or 2 by 6 that is 2 feet longer than the area to be screeded. Cut plywood to the thickness of the pavers plus the width of the board; its length should be about

2 inches less than the area to be screeded. Attach the plywood as shown so that it extends below the board by the thickness of a paver minus ¼ inch.

4 Spread the Sand

Have the sand delivered right to the patio, taking care not to disturb the landscaping fabric, the gravel, or the edging. Spread the sand with a square shovel and a rake until it is slightly higher than its final level. The sand should be a little damp; if at any point it dries out, spray it with a mist of water. Power-tamp the sand (see page 139) and spread more sand to fill in any low spots.

5 Screed

If the screed is longer than 6 feet, do this step with a helper. Starting at one end, move the screed across the patio to smooth the sand. Then set a paver on top of the sand to be sure it is at the correct height. It may help to saw back and forth as you push or pull the screed across the sand. Fill any voids, moisten the sand if needed, and repeat until you achieve a uniformly smooth surface.

6 Run a Guideline

To prepare for laying pavers, stretch a length of mason's line across the patio to serve as a height guide. Pull the line taut so that it does not sag. Attach it with a nail or screw or wrap the line around a temporary stake, as shown.

screeding with pipe guides

If your patio has a solid edging that's the same height as the patio, use the edging as a guide for screeding, as shown on pages 150–51. If you are using invisible edging, or if you will add uneven edging later, either set up temporary 2-by-4 screed guides or use the pipe method shown here.

Excavate and install invisible edging (see page 143). Spread and tamp the gravel, taking special care to form an even surface that is either level or correctly sloped away from the house. Depending on your local soil conditions, you may choose to spread landscaping fabric over the gravel and then lay the pipes on top of the fabric.

1 Lay Out the Pipes

Use plastic (PVC) pipe, which is inexpensive and light and usually sold according to its inside diameter. For a 1-inch-thick layer of sand, use ¾-inch PVC pipe. Cut the pipes to length so that they fit with an inch or so to spare, and space them about 6 feet apart. Lay a long straight board across several pipes to make sure they describe an even surface. Check for level or correct slope; adjust pipes up or down by adding or removing gravel under them.

2 Tamp and Screed

Pour sand into the area and roughly smooth it with a garden rake. Lay a straight 2 by 4 across two or three of the pipes. Press the board firmly onto the pipes and push or pull it across the patio to screed a smooth surface. If the sand dries out, moisten it with a mist of water. Tamp the sand firm and screed again.

3 Fill the Voids

Remove the pipes, taking care not to disturb the surface. Fill the resulting voids with sand and pat the surface smooth. Now you're ready to lay the pavers.

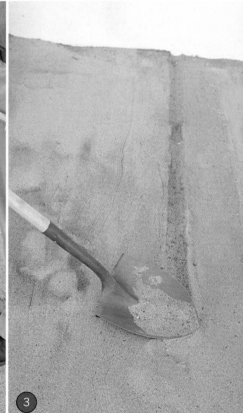

setting pavers in sand

The next two pages give basic instructions for laying pavers in screeded sand following a 90-degree herringbone pattern. For tips on installing other patterns, see pages 155–59. For an overview of the most common paver patterns, see page 101.

As long as you screeded the sand correctly, the pavers you set will be at the right height. However, it is a good idea to stretch mason's line from edging to edging to double-check. If the patio is too high or too low, you may need to remove the pavers and screed again.

1 Lay the First Pavers

Starting in a corner, set several pavers to abut the edging. Use a level or straightedge to see that the pavers are at the desired height. Set each paver straight down onto the bed, gently scraping the side of the edging or an already-laid paver as you lower it; if you slide a paver more than ½ inch or so, you will create waves in the sand and the surface will not be level. Install pavers so that they fit snugly against each other.

2 Bed the Pavers

After you have set 10 or 12 pavers, place a beater board—a flat 2 by 4 or 2 by 6 that is about 2 feet long—on top and tap with a hammer or mallet. If a paver is noticeably higher, tap it directly with the mallet.

MOVING EDGING TO MINIMIZE CUTTING

By adjusting the edging, you may be able to avoid cutting pavers along one or two edges of the patio. Install pavers until you're near the end of the patio, then move the edging to abut them. In the case of 2-by edging (as shown), push the edging up against the pavers and drive stakes and screws to secure it. Use a handsaw or reciprocating saw to cut the adjacent piece of edging flush.

3 Fill in the Patio

As you move across the surface installing pavers, move the guideline with you every 2 feet or so. Until locked in place by edging, bricks can easily be pushed out of position, so if you need to kneel on top of the patio, first put down a piece of plywood large enough to support your toes as well as your knees to evenly distribute your weight.

4 Screed the Other Side

If you installed a temporary screed guide (see page 150, Step 2), work up to it, then screed sand on the other side. Remove the temporary guide, taking care not to disturb the pavers or screeded sand. If the size of your patio requires it, install the guide for a third section. Fill in the void created by removing the temporary guide and screed again, resting one end of the screed on the patio surface. Do this carefully so you do not push any pavers out of position.

5 Fill the Joints

You will likely need to cut some pavers; see pages 147–49. Once all pavers have been installed, pour fine sand over the patio and use a soft-bristled broom to sweep the sand into the joints. If the sand is wet, allow it to dry, then sweep again.

6 Tamp or Spray

Run a vibrating plate compactor over the surface. This will cause the fine sand to settle into the joints. Sweep more sand into the joints and compact again. Alternatively, moisten the patio by spraying it with a mist of water, which will also cause the sand to settle.

quick and easy
installation of a small patio

Interlocking concrete pavers are installed in the same way as rectangular bricks or pavers. However, the following tips will make the job go more smoothly, especially if the patio is small.

- When laying out the patio, skip batterboards and string lines. Instead, measure out a perimeter using a sheet of plywood (which has perfectly square corners) as a guide. Dig a trench and set 2-by-4 edging in place. Check the edging for square with the plywood and stake it in place.

- You may choose to install a single layer of "paver base" instead of a layer of gravel topped with a layer of sand. Paver base is typically sold in fifty-pound bags at home improvement centers.

- Tamp the soil, then the paver base, with a 2 by 4 or a 4 by 4 about 8 feet long. This will take time, but not as much time as two trips to the rental store to rent and return a power tamper. If you tamp carefully, the results will be nearly as firm as those achieved with a vibrating plate compactor.

- To minimize cutting, figure the layout ahead of time.

1 Plan the Cuts
Set the pavers in a dry run to figure out where you need to make your cuts. Ideally, you should have to cut only every other paver on only two sides. When installing "keystone" pavers like these, purchase special perimeter pieces for the edges.

2 Install Edging to Fit
Excavate a somewhat larger area than you need and also cut the edging boards longer than needed. Set the pavers in a dry run and mark where to cut the edging so that you have minimal cutting to do.

3 Set the Pavers
Spread the paver base, tamp and screed it, and set the pavers. If the pavers don't quite fit, unscrew and pull out some stakes and adjust the edging as needed. Once the pavers are installed, cut any overhanging edging ends. Sweep sand into the joints.

Bricks are arranged in a half-basketweave pattern to form a border to the patio. Rows of light-colored bricks define the vegetable beds and allow the gardener to access them from all sides.

installing other patterns

Don't compromise when it comes to the paver pattern. Laying a pattern with a rich texture will require at most only one more day of work than a straightforward pattern—small potatoes compared to all the work you put into excavating and preparing the site. These two pages show some of the most popular patterns.

When installing a pattern that requires pavers that face in several different directions, stand back and examine your work every 15 minutes or so to make sure you didn't make any mistakes. For basic instructions on screeding, setting pavers, filling joints with sand, and tamping, see pages 150–54.

USING A FRAMED GRID

With this method, you first install the wooden grid, then set pavers inside the grid's sections. Each section must be perfectly square (or rectangular) and just the right size to hold a certain number of full-sized pavers. To be safe, estimate the overall size of the patio, then cut the outer edging boards slightly larger than needed. Cut the boards to fit precisely when you construct the grid. Use pressure-treated or other very rot-resistant lumber.

Install wood or timber outside edging and lay a bed of tamped gravel 4 inches below the top of the edging. Build a grid from 2 by 4s. To measure for the grid, lay pavers in a dry run in both directions; use $\frac{1}{4}$-inch spacers to make sure there will be ample room for the pavers. First install a series of 2 by 4s that run the entire length of the patio, then install short boards between them. Fasten the boards by driving $2\frac{1}{2}$-inch deck screws.

Make a short screed that will fit into a grid section. Pour and screed the sand in each section. Lay the pavers in the pattern of your choice.

THE PINWHEEL PATTERN

The half-pavers in the pinwheel pattern can be made from a different material as long as they are the same thickness as the other pavers and no wider than the other pavers. It's all right if they are a bit smaller; the joints can be filled easily with sand.

Set one square—composed of four full pavers and one half-paver—and then move on to the next square. Use a guideline every two or three squares to keep the pattern straight.

THE ANGLED HERRINGBONE

If you install the edging and pavers very accurately, this pattern will enable you to end up with a large number of cuts that are exactly 45 degrees. However, it is likely that things will go slightly out of alignment, so make sure the rented wet saw you use comes with an adjustable saw guide. This will let you tinker with the cutting angles.

Before you screed the sand, measure and mark the exact center of the edging on two parallel sides of the patio. Tack a small nail at one of the marks. After you screed, snap a chalk line in the sand.

With painstaking precision, install a V-shaped row of pavers along the line for about 6 feet. The paver corners should just touch the chalk line. Use an angle square to check the angle; you are establishing the alignment for the whole patio. For succeeding rows, just install pavers tight against each other.

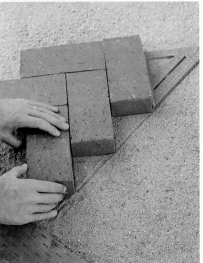

CUTTING IN PLACE

If you want to install a border along one edge or around the perimeter of a patio, you must cut the pavers in a straight line. You could snap a chalk line and then cut each paver individually, but the resulting line may not be as even as you'd like. Another option is to rent a gas-powered masonry cutoff saw and cut the line in one fell swoop. Obtain thorough instructions from the rental staff and practice on scrap pieces before you make the crucial cut. It may help to anchor a straight board to use as a guide.

CIRCULAR PATTERNS

Pavers arranged in circles, fans, or winding curves add warmth and distinction to a patio. Installing these shapes requires extra planning, time, and effort, but most installations can be accomplished with no special skills.

At a brickyard or other masonry supply source, you will likely find ensembles of pavers that are specially sized and shaped for making circles or curves (see top right). When put together in the right order, they result in a circle or fan with uniformly tight joints. Assembly is easy as long as you follow the manufacturer's

directions for correctly placing the puzzle pieces.

To create a custom pattern like the one shown below left, you will need to cut the pieces with two curved edges and two edges that have a certain angle.

If you're a math wiz you can calculate these arcs and angles; most people will do

better if they cut cardboard templates, test them for fit, then trace the outline on the stones.

An informal curved patio made of standard bricks or pavers will have V-shaped joints and imperfect curves, which, like the one shown below, add to the patio's charm. For instructions on laying a patio such as this, see pages 128–29.

MIXED-MATERIAL PATTERNS

If you appreciate a rustic, home-grown style, consider creating a crazy-quilt pattern using just about any material that can last in the ground. Take the time to develop a look that suits your yard and expresses your personality. Often, a few subtle rearrangements can transform a hodgepodge into an artistic grouping.

The edging and subsurface for mixed-material patterns need to be as substantial as those for standard paver patios (see pages 140–54). If materials vary in thickness, it is usually easiest to install the thickest materials first, then add sand and screed for the thinner materials.

BUILDING A CURVED PATH

A path is essentially a long, narrow patio. The options for edging and paving materials, and the building techniques, are employed much the same.

A path with little foot traffic can be as narrow as 2 feet, but in order for two people to pass comfortably, a path should be at least 40 inches wide.

Space the edging so that you can install all full-sized pavers. Set out a row of pavers the desired width of the path. Cut a 2-by-4 spacer to ½ inch longer than the paver run (to accommodate minor discrepancies in size). Use the spacer as shown to check the spacing between the edgings. Every 3 feet or so, position the spacer between the edgings and drive stakes on both sides.

A crowned walk sheds water quickly, ensuring against puddles. Make a screed as described on page 150. Cut a curve in the plywood, as shown; the highest point, in the middle, should be 1 to 1½ inches higher than the ends. Screed the sand and install pavers as you would for a patio. If needed, pull up a stake and adjust the position of the edging. Drive stakes every foot or so before sweeping sand into the joints.

setting pavers with wide joints

Large adobe blocks, concrete stepping-stones, flagstones, and even chunks of used concrete can be set with joints up to 2 inches wide, allowing ample room for crevice plants. (With bricks and small pavers, joints wider than ¾ inch may make the installation look sloppy rather than charming, and large crevice plants will likely cover most of the paver surface.) Larger joints can be filled with fine gravel or rough sand, but you'll achieve a classic look by filling them with soil and adding crevice plants. The larger the pavers, the more lush the crevice plants can be.

You could install a gravel base as for a standard patio, but large, heavy pavers will likely remain stable if set on tamped soil and a 1-inch layer of sand; larger

crevice plants will also grow better if their roots do not need to poke through a layer of gravel. The pavers may become wobbly in time, especially if the crevice plants have strong roots. However, you can easily lift and reset pavers.

Top: Square concrete pavers are set with wide joints on this hillside patio. The grass growing between the pavers enlivens the space, making it the perfect spot to enjoy a morning cup of coffee or juice. *Below:* Loose gravel fills wide joints between geometric-shaped concrete pavers. The variety of potted plants and trees sitting atop this patio lends a casual feel.

1 Plan the Layout

Lay the pavers in a dry run with the desired joint width; if necessary, adjust the joint widths rather than cut the pavers. Place a group of pavers, forming a square of 3 to 4 feet, spaced as you desire. On the edging, measure and mark the center point of every second or third joint. Remove the pavers, add sand, and screed.

2 Set the Pavers

Using the marks made in Step 1, tack small nails and stretch mason's line to form a grid of equal-sized sections; each section will contain a certain number of pavers. Double-check the sizes. Place pavers in one section and fine-tune their placement to achieve joints that are relatively consistent in width. If you need to move a paver, pick it up and set it back down; don't slide it. Use a straight board to check that the pavers are even with each other. If a paver is wobbly, add or remove sand underneath.

3 Fill the Joints

Use a square shovel or a garden trowel to fill the joints with soil appropriate for the crevice plants you have chosen. Because the soil will get tightly compacted, it is often best to mix some sand in with the potting soil to produce soil that is firm but able to drain.

4 Tamp and Plant

Sweep the surface using light strokes. Gently tamp the joints using a board that is slightly thinner than the joints. Sow seeds or add some plants to the joints. Fill with soil and sweep again.

building stairs

I f a slope leads to or from your patio, you may need to build stairs. If the slope is gentle, stair construction can be casual: perhaps excavate a few level spots and position large stone slabs or concrete pavers on them. However, a stairway of three or more steps should be carefully planned so that all steps are consistent and of a comfortable height.

PLANNING THE STEPS

Steps should be at least 2 feet wide. Make them 4 to 5 feet wide if you want two people to walk abreast or have a comfortable place to sit and chat. The treads should be sloped at a rate of about $\frac{1}{4}$ inch per foot so rainwater can easily flow down the stairs or to the side.

A rise—the vertical distance from one stair tread to another—should be between 5 and 8 inches. For a step to be comfortable and safe, the horizontal run—the depth of the tread—plus twice the vertical rise should equal 25 to 27 inches. For instance, if the rise is $5\frac{1}{2}$ inches (the thickness of a 6 by 6), the tread should be around 15 inches ($5\frac{1}{2} \times 2 = 11$, $+15 = 26$). If the rise is greater, then the run must become smaller; a step with a $7\frac{1}{2}$-inch rise requires a run that is approximately 11 inches.

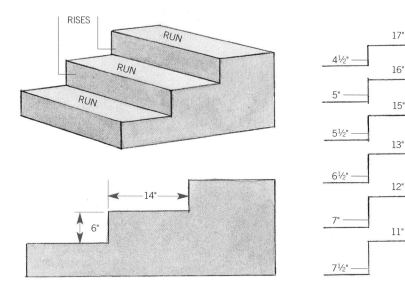

Hold a long, straight board with a level on top and measure down from it to find the stairway's total rise. Divide the total rise by the desired rise height for each step to find out how many steps you need. Then multiply the number of steps by the run for each step to estimate the total length of the stairway.

You may need to adjust the rise or run, or even the number of steps, to make everything come out right. Make a drawing to help you envision the stairway. Make sure the bottom and top steps will be the same height as all the others.

EXCAVATING

For the initial excavation, create an even slope that is approximately the right depth for the front edge of each step minus 2 to 3 inches for the gravel bed. You can perform the second excavation step either before you install the steps (if you are confident of your measuring skills) or as you install the steps. The second step involves digging a series of horizontal areas that follow the contours of the stairway, so that each tread will be supported with a 2-to-3-inch-thick layer of compactible gravel.

TIMBER AND GRAVEL STEPS

Gravel steps are easy to build, and they drain well. Start by building timber frames as shown on pages 164–65. Excavate as you lay the timbers on top of each other and anchor them to the ground by driving pieces of rebar or pipe, then fill the resulting cavities with gravel.

SLAB STAIRS

This type of stairway is easiest to build if you start with massive stone slabs that are similar in thickness, automatically providing steps with fairly consistent rises. The front of each step must rest on and overlap the step below, so the slabs should be at least 3 inches wider than the desired run.

Starting at the top and working downward, use a square shovel to excavate as you lay the slabs.

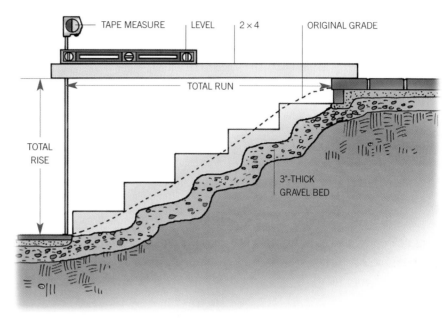

TAPE MEASURE   LEVEL   2 × 4   ORIGINAL GRADE

TOTAL RUN

TOTAL RISE

3"-THICK GRAVEL BED

Left: Timber-and-gravel steps have rough-hewn charm, yet the rises are all exactly the same height, for easy walking. **Below:** Limestone slabs stack to form the steps, and matching flagstones are used for the landings.

Where possible, excavate carefully, so that you can set the slabs on undisturbed soil. If you need to add soil, be sure to tamp it firm before setting a slab on top.

TIMBER AND PAVER STAIRS

A stairway like this is basically a series of small patios with timber edging enclosing a gravel-and-sand bed. A 4-by-6 timber set on edge is 5½ inches high, a good height for a step rise.

See pages 162–63 for planning rise and run and for information on excavating. However, since you can't adjust the rises on this stairway, you may need to excavate or build up the grade at the bottom of the stairway to make the bottom step the same height as the others. Use straight pieces of 4-by-6 pressure-treated lumber that are not deeply cracked.

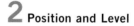

1 Build the Frames

On a flat surface, lay pavers (in whatever pattern you wish) in a dry run to determine the inside dimensions of each frame; you should not need to cut any pavers. Build the frames about ¼ inch larger than needed to compensate for imperfections in the lumber (you can later fill any resulting gaps with sand). Measure and cut the frame pieces using a circular saw. One timber should cross the entire front of each step and the side timbers should butt into it. Fit the rear timbers between the sides. At each joint, drill two pilot holes using a long bit. Then tap a 7-inch lag screw with a washer partway into each hole and tighten all the screws with a socket wrench.

2 Position and Level

Place 2 to 3 inches of compactible gravel at the bottom of the stairway to make the surface 5½ inches below the calculated level for the first step. Tamp with a hand tamper or a 4 by 4. Set the frame for the first step on the tamped gravel and check for level or the correct slope.

3 Install the Frames

Add succeeding frames one at a time, checking each for correct slope and excavating and adding gravel as needed. Once you are certain of the positioning, anchor each frame with four or six pieces of reinforcing bar (or galvanized pipe). Whether the frame piece rests on gravel or on another 4 by 6, drill a hole and drive a piece of rebar 2 to 3 feet long, depending on soil conditions. Driving the rebar should take some effort but should not be a struggle.

4 Tamp and Screed

When all the frames have been installed, check that they are stable. In each frame, pour compactible gravel to a depth of one paver thickness plus $1\frac{1}{2}$ inches lower than the top of the frame. Tamp the gravel with a 2 by 4. Shovel in sand and use a scrap piece of wood to screed the sand so that it is a paver's thickness below the top of the frame.

5 Set the Pavers

Place the pavers into the frames in the pattern of your choice. Tap with a board and a rubber mallet and check with a straight board to see that the pavers form an even surface. Sweep fine sand to fill the joints, spray with a fine mist, and repeat the process once or twice until the sand no longer sinks down when you spray it.

FLAGSTONE STEPS

Timber or lumber frames can also be filled with flagstone or other paving materials. You will probably need to cut some of the stones.

building with concrete and mortar

A concrete slab that is cast correctly will remain rock-solid for many decades; paving materials that are set in mortar on such a slab will be just as durable. This chapter shows how to spruce up an existing slab with coverings of flagstone, pavers, pebbles, or tile as well as how to pour and finish a brand-new slab.

working with mortar

Whether you are installing stones, pavers, or tiles, it is important to get the mortar just right. If mortar is mixed correctly—not too wet, not too dry, with the right proportions of Portland cement and sand—it will be easy to set the paving materials and you can be assured they'll stay stuck.

For setting stones, large stone tiles, and concrete pavers or bricks, buy bags of mortar mix, which is composed of Portland cement mixed with sand. (For a very large job you could buy Portland cement and sand separately and mix them yourself, but the money you'll save is usually not substantial compared to using ready mixed.)

Type N mortar is strong enough for most home masonry projects. Buy Type S if pavers will stay wet for long periods or if you want extra strength. Another way you can add strength is to buy a separate bag of Portland cement and add a shovel or two to each bag of mortar mix.

It is usually easiest to mix mortar in a wheelbarrow or a large masonry trough. Dump in a full bag of mortar mix, then gradually add water while you mix with a mason's hoe, shovel, or standard hoe. For most purposes, mortar is the right thickness when you can cut ridges in it with a trowel and the ridges

hold their shape. The mortar is too dry if it appears crumbly. Another way to test is to scoop up some mortar with a trowel and hold it upside down. The mortar should stick to the trowel for a second or two. If it is too dry, add water; if it's too wet, add dry mix.

The right mortar thickness can depend on what you are laying as well as on the current temperature and humidity. For large, heavy stones, the mix should be fairly stiff—just wet enough so that the mortar sticks to the stones. If the air is hot and dry, make the mix wetter; then check from time to time to make sure the pavers are sticking. If conditions are very dry, you may need to dip the pavers in water before setting them.

Keep your batch of mortar in the shade; direct sunlight will dry it quickly. After two hours (sooner if the air is hot and dry), the mortar will begin to harden. If lumps appear or the mortar becomes generally stiff, throw it out and mix a new batch.

In a warm climate, you can fill joints between the pavers using the dry-mortar method: after the pavers are set, dry-mix 1 part mortar mix with 4 parts sand and sweep the mixture into joints; take care to sweep the pavers clean. Spray the patio with a fine mist of water, taking care to avoid making puddles. Finish the joints with a masonry jointer, as shown on page 179.

For installing tiles smaller than 16 inches square, use latex- or polymer-reinforced thinset mortar; see page 173.

setting flagstones on a concrete slab

A mortared flagstone surface is easier to keep clean than soil-laid flagstone (see pages 122–23) and also more permanent. You can lay a new slab for mortaring the flagstone (pages 182–86), but you can also use an existing one. The slab should be in sound condition; see page 76. Mortaring stones on top of a slab will give the structure additional strength.

If you want to install edging for this project, you will need to cut most of the stones around the perimeter—which is probably not worth the trouble. Instead, you can allow the stones to overhang the slab for a pleasantly uneven edge.

CHOOSING AND SORTING STONES

See pages 98–99 for tips on selecting flagstone. For an easier installation, buy stones that are at least close to uniform in thickness.

This flagstone-on-concrete patio uses large pieces of brown and gray sandstone, which look right at home in a wide-open setting. The joints are filled with white mortar, which contrasts strongly with the flagstones and emphasizes their shapes.

Have the stones delivered near the site. Sort them into three or four piles according to size. When you lay the stones out, choose some from each pile so that you end up with a fairly even distribution of the large, medium, and small stones.

1 Apply Bonding Agent

Scrub the slab free of any oily deposits with a garage floor cleaner or a mild muriatic-acid solution; rinse thoroughly. To make certain that the mortar will stick to the concrete, brush liquid concrete bonding agent over the slab following the manufacturer's directions. Usually, you need to wait for the bonding agent to dry partially and then apply the mortar within a few hours.

2 Mix the Mortar

Avoid working when the sun is shining directly on the job site; strong sunlight will cause the mortar to dry quickly. At the least, keep the wheelbarrow or mixing trough in the shade. Following the general directions on page 167, mix a batch of mortar that is fairly stiff yet wet enough to stick to the stones and the slab.

3 Set a Large Stone

On a small patio, you can skip this step; shovel out mortar and begin arranging stones. To provide a reference point for height and to help ensure an even distribution of large stones, shovel out mortar and set a large, thick stone near the middle of an area that is about 8 feet square. Check that the area is fairly level (or sloped in the direction that the slab is sloped) in both directions.

4 Arrange the Layout

Expect to spend most of your time arranging, re-arranging, and reorienting stones in a pleasing pattern. Work with helpers and rest often to avoid hurting your back. Fill in a 4-foot-square area around the large stone with dry-laid stones. (Adjust the position of the reference stone if that helps the layout.) Aim for joints that are roughly uniform in width, and avoid having any stones touch each other. If some stones vary in color and texture, also aim to distribute them fairly evenly. In some cases, you will need to mark some stones for cutting.

5 Cut Stones As Needed

If you cut with a chisel, expect stones to break the way you want them to about 60 percent of the time; the rest of the time, they will choose their own course. If you're not happy with a cut, grab another stone and try again. Wear protective eye gear because shards of stone will fly. Move the stone to an area where you can easily sweep away the shards. Cut with a chisel following the instructions on page 147. For a more accurate cut, you may choose to score a line about ½ inch deep with a circular saw or a grinder and then break the piece off with a sledge. To make a cut line appear natural, tap it all along its length with a sledge or a masonry hammer.

6 Apply Mortar

Every 10 minutes or so, use a shovel or hoe to remix the mortar. If it starts to stiffen, add a little more water. If it stays stiff or starts to develop hard chunks, throw it out and mix a new batch.

Set the thickest stones first, then the thinner stones. Pick up one or two of the dry-laid stones and set them to the side, oriented so you can easily replace them in the correct position. Shovel some mortar onto the concrete and use a trowel to roughly even it out. For thin stones, apply a thicker layer of mortar.

7 Bed the Stones

With practice and plenty of trial and error, you can produce a stone surface that is reasonably level. Set the stones in the mortar and check that each is close to level and about the same height as its neighbors. Every few stones, use a straight board to check the height. Make any needed adjustments right away, before the mortar starts to set. If a stone is low, remove it, apply more mortar, and reset it. If a stone is too high, tap it down and scrape away the excess mortar that oozes out.

8 Fill Between the Stones

Wait a day or so for the mortar to set. Slip mortar into the gaps between stones using a mason's trowel or a mortar's bag (see page 179). Work carefully to get as little mortar on the stones' surfaces as possible. For an even fill, gently scrape off excess with a small piece of wood. After the mortar has started to dry, lightly brush away crumbs.

For a more natural look, fill the joints with fine crushed stone, as shown. To keep the gravel from seeping out when you clean the patio, mix 1 part Portland cement with 3 parts gravel. After checking that the stones are completely dry, to prevent mortar from smearing on them, brush the stones into the joints. Sweep in several directions to work the stones in deeply between the flagstones. You may need to pick up some larger stones if they get caught in a narrow space.

9 Clean and Rinse

Once you have swept the stones completely clean, spray the surface using a garden hose with the nozzle set on mist. Stop spraying once puddles begin to form. Wait for the stones to dry, then repeat. Use a damp rag to carefully scrub away any mortar smears. If you end up with a mortar "haze," allow the patio to dry and wash with a mild muriatic acid solution. To make the stones easy to keep clean and to give them a slightly wet look, apply a coat or two of acrylic sealer.

OTHER OPTIONS FOR FILLING JOINTS

If you don't like the look of mortar- or gravel-filled joints, you can brush in sand instead. The sand will likely wash away in time, but you can easily add more later. Use rough sand, sometimes called torpedo sand.

While the joints are not deep enough to support most plants, you can fill them with sandy soil and apply a moss slurry; see page 66.

Strips of blue glazed tiles run through a field of terra-cotta tiles. A stunning design like this calls for plenty of careful planning and precise cutting, and is probably best left to the pros.

tiling over concrete

Ceramic tiles are typically 12 inches square or smaller, making them an ideal choice for a small patio. Choose tiles that are made to withstand your climate and that will provide slip resistance (see pages 104–5). The Mexican Saltillos shown in this project are popular in the West and Southwest but may not hold up in other areas.

Because they are handmade and irregular in shape and size, tiles like these should be set in a grid, so you can adjust for discrepancies. If you are installing tiles that are precisely sized, you could set the first tiles along two perpendicular layout lines and use plastic spacers to maintain precise grout lines.

Large tiles are often set in 3-feet-square sections, each of which holds nine tiles. Test that this arrangement will result in grout lines the width that you want. (On an exterior installation, grout lines that are as wide as ³⁄₈ to ¹⁄₂ inch are the norm.) Lay three tiles next to each other on a flat surface, spaced as you like them. Measure the width of the three tiles and add the width of one grout line; this is the size of the squares in which the tiles should be laid.

Purchase a square-notched trowel of a size recommended by the tile manufacturer—usually ¹⁄₄ inch by ¹⁄₄ inch or ¹⁄₄ inch by ³⁄₈ inch.

1 Plan the Layout

Check the slab for square (see page 136). If it is out of square, draw square lines and make all your measurements from the lines. Measure the length and width of the installation and divide by the chosen width of the sections (as described above). Plan your installation so that you avoid having narrow cut tiles at any edge. In both directions along the slab, make a V-shaped mark every 3 feet or at every multiple of the chosen width for the squares.

2 Snap Grid Lines

Snap one chalk line going in each direction and check the resulting corner to make sure it is square; make adjustments in the marks if necessary. Snap all the lines to produce a grid of squares on the entire surface to be tiled. Double-check that the squares are all the same size; it's easy to make mistakes.

3 Apply Mortar

Purchase bags of thinset mortar. The thinset should be reinforced either with dry polymers (in which case you simply mix it with water) or by mixing it with liquid latex. Mix in a bucket, either with an electric drill equipped with a mixing paddle or by hand using a margin trowel. The mortar should be fairly wet but stiff enough so that the lines produced by a notched trowel hold their shape.

Using the flat side of a trowel, spread a thick coat—about 1 inch—inside one of the squares. Take care not to cover up the working lines. Spread with long, sweeping strokes to produce a surface that is fairly level.

4 Comb the Mortar

Use the notched side of the trowel to comb the surface of the mortar. The notches should scrape the concrete only rarely, if ever. Work to create an even surface with no globs or gaps.

CUTTING ROUGH TILES

Some tiles can be cut with a snap cutter, a simple hand tool that you can buy or rent. For tiles that cannot be cut with a snap cutter, rent a wet saw if you need to cut a lot of them. If you need to cut only a few tiles, you can use a circular saw or a grinder equipped with a masonry blade. In the example shown here, a clamped 1 by 2 is used as a guide. It will take several passes to cut about halfway through a tile; then you can snap it to finish the cut.

5 Place the Tiles

If the tiles are reasonably flat, you can simply set them in the mortar. If they are very rough or warped, you may need to first apply a thin coat of mortar (a process called back-buttering) to the back of each before setting it. Set each tile straight down into the mortar; avoid sliding a tile more than ½ inch or so. Place the outer tiles so that they are half a joint line away from the layout lines. Once you have placed all nine tiles, stand back and examine the joints from several angles. The lines will not be perfect, but they should be close; make adjustments as needed.

6 Bed and Check Adhesion

Gently tap the tiles with a hammer over a block of wood to embed them in the mortar and create a smooth surface. In every square, pick up at least one tile to make sure the mortar is sticking to three-quarters or more of its back surface. If not, back-butter the tiles.

Use small pieces of wood or strips of cardboard to scrape away any mortar that oozes up in the joints; all the joints should be at least ¼ inch deep to accommodate the grout (see the next step). Immediately clean up any mortar smears on the tiles with a clean, damp rag.

7 Apply the Grout

Allow the mortar to harden; this may take two days if the weather is not dry. Purchase sanded grout of a color that blends with the tiles. Mix a batch of grout that is just barely pourable and pour some onto the tile surface. Holding a laminated grout float nearly flat, push the grout into the grout lines using sweeping back-and-forth strokes. At every point, be sure to push the grout with strokes running in two or more directions. Then tip the float up and use it like a squeegee to scrape away most of the grout from the surface of the tiles.

Move the float across the tiles diagonally so that the edge of the float does not dig into any joints.

Once you've applied grout to an area about 8 square feet, wipe the surface gently with a damp towel or a large sponge; take care to keep the grout at a consistent depth. Repeat, rinsing the towel or sponge often in clean water, until the tiles are clean. Allow the grout to dry, then buff the surface with a dry cloth. If a grout haze remains, clean it with a mild muriatic acid solution.

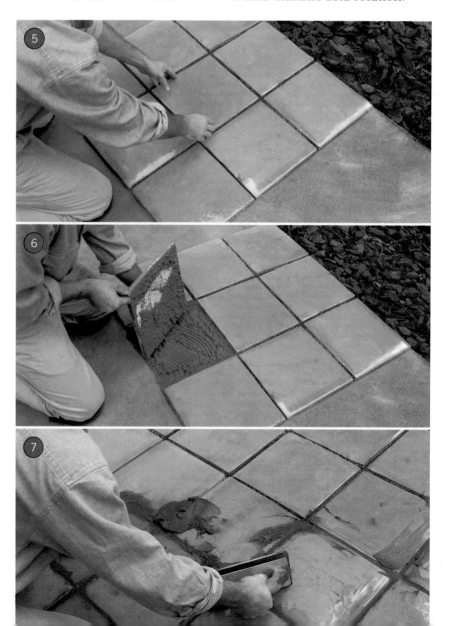

SETTING SMALL TILES

Smaller tiles add rich texture, making them a good choice for a modest-sized patio or a set of concrete stairs. They result in more grout lines, which improve skid resistance, making it practical to install glazed tiles. For a patio, you will likely use only field tiles, which have unfinished edges; the edges will not be very visible. On a stairway or another area where edges will be on display, use bullnose tiles, which have one edge that is rounded off and finished.

Before you mix the mortar, lay the tiles in a dry run on the concrete in the same way they will appear in the finished job. Use plastic spacers to maintain consistent joints. See that all the joints—including any between horizontal and vertical tiles—are the same width. Cut tiles as needed using a snap cutter or a wet saw.

Follow the instructions on pages 172–74 for inspecting the slab, mixing thinset mortar, using a beater board, and inspecting tiles for mortar coverage.

1 Apply Thinset

Once you are sure of your layout, mix and apply thinset mortar using a square-notched trowel. Spread a flat, even surface with no gaps or globs. You can correct minor holes and dips in the concrete as you trowel. Trowel on a small area and apply the tiles; later, as you gain confidence, you can work on larger areas.

2 Set the Tiles

Set any vertical tiles first. If necessary, support them with plastic spacers or folded pieces of cardboard to keep them from sliding down. Then install the horizontal pieces that overlap the verticals (these may be bullnose pieces). To create consistent grout lines, you may need to adjust some of the vertical tiles or raise the height of some horizontal tiles by picking them up and adding more mortar underneath. Press each tile into the mortar with a slight twist; avoid sliding a tile more than $\frac{1}{2}$ inch. Install spacers as you lay the tiles. Tap with a beater board to achieve an even surface.

3 Grout and Clean

Allow the tiles to set overnight at least, until the thinset is not only hard but has lightened in color, indicating that it is mostly cured. Mix grout and apply with a laminated float. Use a large rag or sponge to wipe away excess mortar and to tool the joints to a consistent depth. Wipe several times, rinsing the rag with clean water each time.

setting pebbles in mortar

Simple pebbles or decorative elements such as tile or glass shards can be assembled in patterns that resemble a tapestry or an oriental carpet. The work is painstaking, but requires no special skills. Set the job up so you can work on one small area at a time.

PREPARING THE SUBSURFACE

The base for the pebbles must be firm. A solid concrete slab (see page 76) is ideal. If you live in an area where the ground doesn't freeze, you can install pebbles in mortar on a 3- or 4-inch-thick bed of firmly compacted gravel or paver base.

You will need permanent edging that is at least 2 inches high. Make sure that the area is slightly sloped for drainage; water that puddles and freezes can cause the pebbles to pop out.

CHOOSING AND SORTING PEBBLES

Choose pebbles that will look good whether they are wet or dry. If you prefer the wet look, coat the pebbles with acrylic sealer when the job is finished.

A home center will carry a small selection of pebbles; check out a stone yard for a wider variety. Pebbles of any type usually vary in color, so you may want to

buy a large quantity and then sort them. Pebbles are often plentiful along rivers or in fields. Because they are small, there is usually no problem if you harvest a modest amount from public land.

Choose pebbles that will present a flat face when laid in mortar. You will probably want to use different sizes; a good mix might be a few accent stones as large as a foot in diameter, a good number of pebbles that are 2 to 3 inches

in diameter, and some smaller stones for filler.

Sort the stones by color in buckets or trays for easy access. Lay some pebbles out on a flat surface to see how many of each color you need. If you like, cut a piece of plywood to the size of the area to be filled with pebbles and lay the pebbles on the plywood in a dry run. You can then easily transfer the pebbles to the mortar in the same configuration.

1 Set the Larger Pebbles

Work when the area is in shade so the mortar does not dry quickly. Mix a fairly wet batch of thinset mortar (see page 173), pour it into the area, and smooth it so it is about ½ inch below the top of the edging. Push each stone into the mortar so that at least two-thirds of it is embedded. Each stone should feel stuck—there should be definite resistance if you try to pull it out. If the stones don't stick, they may be too dry; dip each briefly in water before setting it. As you work, you may have to add mortar or scoop mortar out to maintain a fairly consistent height. If the mortar starts to stiffen, throw it out and mix a new batch.

2 Set More Pebbles

For some patterns, you will want to poke each pebble individually into the mortar. If the pattern involves very small stones, you may choose to sprinkle them onto the mortar. It often looks good to lay some pebbles flat and others on edge.

3 Bed the Pebbles

Before the mortar in the area you are working on starts to harden—about 15 minutes or so—lay a piece of plywood over it and step on it. Depending on the hardness of the mortar, step gingerly, give it your full weight, or even jump on the board. This will embed the stones in the mortar and help create a relatively level surface.

The stones should sink slightly lower than needed for the finished appearance; some surface mortar will be washed away in the next step.

4 Clean the Surface

Once the mortar has begun to harden, spray the stones with a fine mist to remove any spattered mortar. If you need to brush the pebbles, use a soft brush or cloth and work gently. Cover the area with plastic and keep it moist so the mortar can cure slowly over several days. If after curing the stones are covered with a mortar haze, clean with a mild solution of muriatic acid. If any of the pebbles come loose, glue them back in place with thinset mortar.

paving over concrete

A solid concrete slab (see page 76) can be paved over with bricks or concrete pavers. This job does call for patient attention to detail, especially when filling the joints (Steps 3 and 4), but does not require special masonry skills.

The resulting patio will be 4 inches or so higher than the concrete. As a result, you may need to raise the level of the surrounding lawn by cutting away some sod, adding soil, and replacing sod. Or, install a flower bed border around the patio.

Set the pavers in any pattern that you choose; see page 101 for ideas. Lay the pavers in a dry run on the concrete; you may choose to adjust the thickness of the joint lines or allow the pavers to hang over the slab by an inch or so if that will reduce the number of cuts you need to make. Install permanent edging or temporary forms that are higher than the slab by the thickness of a paver plus ½ inch (¼ inch for the underlying mortar; pavers should end up sitting ¼ inch above the edging).

1 Screed the Mortar

Clean the slab and apply latex bonding agent (see page 169). Make a screed out of a 2 by 4 or 2 by 6 and a piece of plywood (see page 150); the plywood should extend downward ¼ inch less than the thickness of a paver.

Mix the mortar, following the instructions on page 167. For extra strength, add a shovelful of Portland cement to each bag of dry-mix mortar. The mortar should be just wet enough to pour and should cling firmly to a trowel. Shovel the mortar onto the slab and smooth it with the screed guide (see page 184 for screeding tips).

2 Bed the Bricks

Using scraps of ½- or ⅜-inch plywood as spacers, set the pavers in the mortar. The bricks should feel stuck when you lay them; if not, you may need to spray or dip the bricks in water before setting them. Lay a flat board on top of them and tap with a hammer to bed the pavers and produce a flat surface. You should see the underlying mortar begin to ooze upward in the joints, but it should not rise to the surface.

3 Fill the Joints

Wait a day for the mortar to harden. Mix a small new batch of mortar and use a trowel to scoop it into a grout bag (also called a mortar bag). Working carefully, squeeze the bag—folding it when needed—to squirt mortar into the joints. Fill the joints completely without smearing the bricks.

4 Finish the Joints

Once the mortar is just hard enough to hold the shape of your finger when you press on it, use a brick jointer to finish the joints. Press the jointer into each joint and scrape gently back and forth until you achieve a smooth surface. Tool the long joints first, then the short ones. If tooling produces crumbs on any bricks, leave them alone and allow them to dry. However, if mortar smears on the bricks, wipe it immediately with a damp cloth.

5 Brush and Clean

When the mortar is fairly dry, brush it lightly with a mason's brush. Take care not to brush any wet mortar or you will smear it. Use a jointer or your finger to fill in any voids or holes with mortar. After several hours, clean the surface using a mason's brush and water. After a week or so, apply acrylic sealer to the entire surface.

179

figuring concrete needs

Pouring a concrete slab is definitely the most ambitious project in this book, especially if the slab is large. Not only is the work physically demanding, all of the operations must be well planned and performed in a timely manner, before the project is "set in concrete." Before you start, be sure you understand how a slab is constructed and how to calculate your concrete needs.

ANATOMY OF A SLAB

To remain free of cracks, a concrete slab must rest on a stable subsurface—typically, a 4- or 5-inch-thick layer of compactible gravel that has been compressed with a vibrating plate compactor (see page 139). Firmly staked forms, usually made of 2 by 4s, hold the concrete in place while it is poured.

The concrete itself should meet local codes for strength and should be at least 3 inches thick for a patio or walkway. To contain cracking, concrete is often reinforced with 6-inch wire mesh, as shown. However, wire mesh is sold only in very large rolls, which makes it impractical for a home-owner. As long as your local building code allows it, we recommend that you order concrete with fiberglass reinforcement.

This reinforcement is at least as effective as wire mesh, costs a modest amount, and makes the installation easier. In some areas, a fibrous isolation joint is required where the slab meets the house; in other areas, it is not recommended.

HOW WILL IT BE FINISHED?

A broom finish (see Step 18, page 186) provides traction and is within the capabilities of do-it-yourselfers. If you want a very smooth surface, hire a professional finisher to finish the concrete with a steel trowel.

It is worth your while to practice producing a smooth broom finish. Make a 4-by-6-foot frame from 2 by 4s and attach it to a piece of plywood. Mix a 60-pound bag of concrete with water and pour it into the frame. Screed and finish the concrete as described on pages 184–86.

UNDERSTANDING CONCRETE

Concrete is composed of Portland cement, sand, gravel (also called aggregate), and water. Portland cement is the glue; the more of it, the stronger the concrete. When ordering from a ready-mix company, specify how much cement you want. A "seven-bag mix" contains seven bags of concrete per cubic yard of concrete—strong enough for most projects.

The mix should contain enough water so that you can easily pour and work it; too much

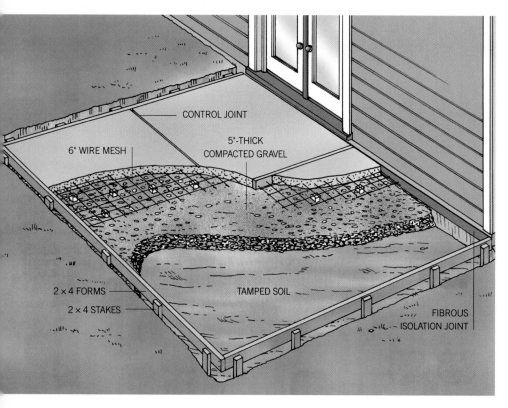

CONTROL JOINT

5"-THICK COMPACTED GRAVEL

6" WIRE MESH

2 × 4 FORMS

2 × 4 STAKES

TAMPED SOIL

FIBROUS ISOLATION JOINT

water weakens the concrete and causes cracks. An inspector may test concrete for "slump" with a special testing cone to see that it is not too soupy and not too dry. Gravel and sand should also be in the right proportion. If dirt gets into a concrete mix, the concrete will be weakened.

If you live in an area that has freezing winters, be sure to order air-entrained concrete, which contains tiny bubbles that add flexibility and make the concrete less likely to crack. If the concrete might freeze during the pour or a few days afterward, have accelerator added; this makes the concrete harden faster. If the weather is hot and dry, have re-tardant added; this will slow the drying process and buy you enough time to properly finish the surface.

CALCULATING HOW MUCH YOU NEED

Concrete is sold by the cubic yard, also just called a "yard." A yard fills an area 3 feet by 3 feet by 3 feet. For small projects, you may choose to measure cubic footage instead. A 60-pound bag of concrete mix produces $\frac{1}{2}$ cubic foot; a 90-pound bag yields $\frac{2}{3}$ cubic foot. (There are 27 cubic feet in a yard.)

To calculate the area, multiply width in feet times length in feet. To figure the area for a circular slab, multiply the radius in feet squared times pi (3.14). If the

patio is an irregular shape, divide it into rectangles and portions of circles, as shown below. Measure the thickness, in inches, in a number of spots to obtain a reliable average; a discrepancy of $\frac{1}{2}$ inch can make a big difference in the amount of concrete you need. With these two figures—area plus thickness—a supplier can quickly calculate your concrete needs.

To figure it yourself, grab a calculator. Multiply area in feet times thickness in inches. Divide the result by 12 to get the number of cubic feet. Divide that number by 27 to get the number of cubic yards. For example, if a slab measures 12 feet by 14 feet, it covers 168 square feet. If the slab is $3\frac{1}{2}$ inches thick:

$$168 \times 3.5 = 588$$
$$588 \div 12 = 49 \text{ cubic feet}$$
$$49 \div 27 = 1.8 \text{ cubic yards}$$

Add approximately 10 percent for waste and order 2 yards.

ORDER OR MIX IT YOURSELF?

For a slab that needs less than $\frac{1}{2}$ yard (or $13\frac{1}{2}$ cubic feet), you may choose to mix bags of concrete in a wheelbarrow. However, be sure to work in small sections or have plenty of help on hand so you can mix quickly; otherwise, you may have trouble finishing the concrete before it hardens. For moderate amounts of concrete you could rent a power mixer and have the dry ingredients— the cement, the gravel, and the sand—delivered to the site. But the cost saving is usually not worth the trouble; it is probably better to have the concrete delivered by a ready-mix company.

Many concrete companies, however, do not want to bother delivering any quantity less than a yard. Others have special trucks designed to mix smaller amounts at the job site. Call to find a company to meet your needs.

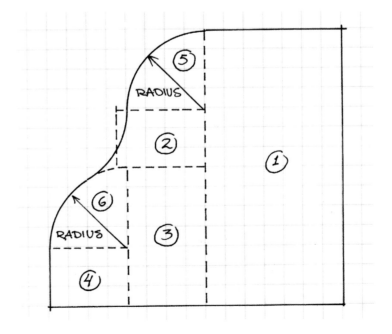

pouring a concrete slab

Before you order concrete to be delivered, carefully read through the steps on pages 182–86; you won't have time to read once the work begins. You will likely need to pay extra if the truck driver has to wait more than half an hour, so be ready to move quickly and get your ducks in a row:

- Have all tools on hand (some you may rent) and two or more reliable helpers.
- Line up a professional finisher if you want a smooth finish.
- Install all the form boards plus any isolation joints and wire reinforcement.
- Lay and test the wheelbarrow paths.
- If you got a permit, arrange for the inspector to be on hand to do any necessary tests, both before and during the pour.

1 Excavate and Build the Form

Lay out the site, remove sod, and measure for correct depth (see pages 138–39). Build the form out of 2 by 4s as you would construct lumber edging (pages 140–41). If the form will be permanent, use pressure-treated or other rot-resistant lumber. Anchor the form boards with some stakes every few feet. Drive the stakes slightly below the top of the form boards. The boards should feel solid when you kick them outward.

2 Frame a Curve

If the form will be permanent, install bender board where you want a curve (see page 141). If the form is temporary, two thicknesses of fibrous isolation membrane make for an easier installation. (You can easily smooth the edges later.)

3 Add a Middle Screed Guide

If the form is wider than 8 feet, it will be difficult to screed across its entire width. Install a temporary screed guide in the middle. Anchor the guide with a stake near the house and drive screws through the form at the other end. This will allow you to remove the guide later on (Step 9).

4 Spread and Tamp Gravel

Use a garden rake or a gravel spreader (as shown) to spread gravel at a consistent depth below the top of the form. Tamp the gravel firm using a vibrating plate compactor, hand tamper, or length of 4 by 4.

5 Build Wheelbarrow Paths

Decide where the concrete truck will park and plan how the concrete will get poured into the formed area. If you're lucky, a chute extension can be added to the truck to pour the concrete directly into the formed area. In most cases, however, you will need to deliver it with wheelbarrows. To keep from damaging your lawn and to provide a smooth running surface for the wheelbarrows, construct paths made of 2 by 10s or 2 by 12s. Use scrap pieces to make a stable bridge wherever the wheelbarrow will go over a form board. Make sure the form will not get bumped as you wheel over the bridge.

6 Pour into Wheelbarrows

It usually works best to have two wheelbarrow operators and one shoveler, who wears heavy boots and remains in the formed area. Set the wheelbarrows on a stable surface under the truck's chute and place a foot on the wheelbarrow's rear frame to keep it from tipping. Tell the driver to pour the first wheelbarrow half full; you may want heavier loads later. Use a scrap of lumber to scrape the chute after it stops pouring so no concrete spills.

7 Wheel and Pour into the Forms

Wheel a load of concrete carefully; it's easy to tip it over if you have not practiced. If you start to lose control of the wheelbarrow, don't try to right it. Instead, push down on the handles with both hands. Then pick up the handles and try again. If you continue to have trouble, ask the driver for smaller loads. Wheel the concrete into a far corner of the formed area and pour it out. Have the shoveler scrape the wheelbarrow, then go back for more.

8 Move Concrete and Screed

Have the shoveler spread the concrete until it is even with, or slightly above, the top of the form boards. Set a straight 2 by 4 on the form board and on the temporary screed guide and work with a helper to screed the concrete by dragging the 2 by 4 across the surface. It may help to move the board in a sawing motion as you pull it.

Where the concrete is low, sprinkle on small amounts of concrete with a shovel, then screed again.

9 Remove the Temporary Screed Guide

If you installed a temporary screed guide, fill and screed one section, then use a shovel to pry out the temporary guide.

10 Screed the Other Side

Working with a helper, screed the other side of the slab. You can let one end of the 2 by 4 rest on the screeded concrete while the other rests on a form board. Fill in any low spots and screed again.

Be sure the form is completely full before saying good-bye to the driver. (He may help you spray-clean your wheelbarrow if you've gotten friendly.) It's a good idea to pour some leftover concrete into a 5-gallon bucket; you may find that you need a little more when you finish the surface.

11 Level with a Bull Float

Leveling a large area is difficult without a bull float; it's a tool well worth renting. Gently set the bull float in the concrete near you and push it forward with the front edge slightly raised. Pull it back over the same area with a series of tugs that produce slight ripples in the concrete—this motion will push stones down and fill in small holes. After each back-and-forth stroke, pick the float up and level the adjacent section with the same motions. Overlap the strokes slightly to make sure you float the entire surface.

12 Smooth with a Magnesium Float

Bull floating will cause "bleed water" (sometimes called "cream") to rise to the surface. Avoid working the surface with any type of float or trowel when there are standing pools of water.

Some finishers use a wood float at this point, but most do-it-yourselfers find a magnesium float easier to use. As soon as the surface is free of puddles, use a magnesium float to further smooth the surface. Start floating at the far corner and work back so that you do not kneel on newly floated concrete. Hold the tool so that the leading edge is slightly raised, and press down gently as you work.

Where you cannot reach across a slab, place two pieces of plywood, each about 2 feet square and screwed to 1-by-2 handles (to make the plywood easy to pick up), on the concrete. One piece is for your knees and one is for your feet. When you need to move, pick up the foot piece and kneel on it, and put the piece that was under your knees under your feet.

13 Cut the Edges

Slip a mason's trowel between the inside of the form boards and the concrete and slice all along the perimeter of the slab. This will eliminate the pockets of air that can weaken the concrete.

14 Tap the Form Boards

To further eliminate air pockets and to help separate the form boards from the concrete, tap the form boards with a hammer all along their length.

15 Round the Edges

Run an edging tool along the outside edges and both sides of any permanent wood dividers. Use back-and-forth sawing motions at first, and then long, sweeping motions to achieve a neatly rounded edge at all points. If air pockets appear, it may help to fill them in with small amounts of leftover wet concrete.

16 Cut a Control Joint

To prevent unsightly cracking, make a control joint in the middle of any section of patio wider than 10 feet. Set a straight 2 by 4 on top of the concrete as a guide. Run the jointer back and forth several times until the concrete is smooth on either side of the joint.

17 Smooth Again

If you have opted for a broom finish (next step), use a magnesium float again to gently smooth the lines produced when you used the jointer and the edger. If you want a smoother finish, have an experienced finisher use a steel trowel to produce a "hard finish." The professional will run the trowel across the surface in wide, sweeping arcs with a moderate amount of pressure, barely bringing moisture to the surface.

18 Broom Finish and Cure

Using a soft-bristled push broom, pull the broom toward you—never push it—to produce a lightly textured surface. If the bristles don't dig in and produce the surface you like, try wetting the broom. Work carefully and aim to produce a consistent texture with straight lines. Avoid overlapping the strokes; make them right next to each other.

The more slowly concrete cures, the stronger it will be. Keep the finished concrete moist for at least a week. Cover the slab with plastic or spray it with a fine mist twice a day (or more often if the air is dry). After a day, carefully pry away the temporary forms.

decorative effects for concrete

If you are confident of your abilities to pour a basic slab (see pages 182–86), you can add a decorative finish as you pour without a lot of extra work. Try the following techniques on a small area first, and move on to larger sections only when you feel comfortable. You can also decorate concrete by pouring a plain slab first and acid-staining or painting it after it has cured (see pages 78–81).

COLORED CONCRETE

A ready-mix concrete company may tint concrete for you for a fee. Typically, they dump a bag of colorant into the top of the truck's mixer to make the entire batch exactly the same color. Make sure the driver does not add water to the concrete after starting to pour because it will change the color.

To color your own concrete, mix a bottle of colorant or a pre-determined amount of powdered color with one or two gallons of water; then add the resulting mixture to two bags of dry-mix concrete. To achieve consistent color, be sure to mix every batch using exactly the same amounts of colorant, water, and dry mix.

A FLAGSTONE DESIGN

This technique is much easier to use on a path or small patio that you can reach across, but you can do it on a larger patio if you start in a far corner and work back toward the edge, finishing each section before you move your kneeling boards (see page 185). You can apply a design like this to colored concrete or wait for plain concrete to cure and then acid-stain each of the sections with two or more colors.

To engrave lines in the concrete, use a brick jointer (it's designed for tooling joints in a brick wall) or a slightly bent piece of ½-inch copper pipe. After you have floated the concrete with a magnesium float (see page 185), wait until the bleed water just disappears and use the jointer or pipe to draw an informal pattern of straight and curved lines. Distribute small and large lines throughout the slab.

Gently run a magnesium float over the surface to knock down most of the crumbs and embed any exposed gravel. Then use a paintbrush or a mason's brush to clear away any remaining crumbs and to produce a finely textured broom finish that extends over the entire surface.

SEEDED AGGREGATE

This process takes longer than adding a standard broom finish, so give yourself plenty of time; you may want to arrange for a retardant to be added to the concrete to give you more time to work.

Exposed aggregate is available in bags; colors usually run from brown to light tan. To add more interest, buy smaller amounts of colored stones as well and scatter the stones sparsely across the surface. Buy plenty of aggregate because you'll really be stuck if you run out.

1 Broadcast the Aggregate
Pour and screed the concrete; you do not need to float it, but make sure all voids are filled and the surface is flat and even. As soon as the bleed water has mostly disappeared, use a shovel or your hand to scatter aggregate over the entire surface; aim for a single layer. You may choose to sprinkle the area with colorful stones as well, and perhaps even embed several large stones for accent.

2 Embed and Float
If the slab is large or the air is dry and hot, cover the part of the slab you're not working on with plastic to keep it wet. Use a flat board or piece of plywood to press the stones well into the concrete. Then work the surface with a magnesium float so that a thin layer of cement without any

gravel in it works its way up and barely covers the stones. Avoid overworking; produce as little bleed water as possible. Use an edger to round off the perimeter and perhaps a jointer to produce control joints (see page 186).

3 Spray and Brush
When the concrete has begun to harden, spray it with a fine mist and brush away the top layer of cement using a broom or a

mason's brush. Stop once the tops of the aggregate are exposed. If stones start coming loose, stop brushing and wait for the concrete to harden further before you start again. After a few hours, spray with a stronger blast of water to fully expose the stones. Allow the slab to cure slowly. If a haze is present after the concrete is fully cured, you can wash the surface with a mild muriatic acid solution.

resources

Cal Spas
(800) 225-7727
Pomona, CA
www.calspas.com
Prefab barbecues, gazebos, firepits

Dig Corporation
(800) 344-2281
Vista, CA
www.digcorp.com
Microsprinklers and drip systems

Gloster Furniture, Inc.
(888) 456-7837
South Boston, VA
www.gloster.com
Outdoor furniture and accessories

**Grupo Kettal
North America, Inc.**
(786) 552-9002
Coral Gables, Florida
www.kettalgroup.com
Outdoor furniture and accessories

Koolfog
(760) 321-9203
Cathedral City, CA
www.koolfog.com
Outdoor misting systems

**Lamps Plus
America's Lighting Superstore**
(800) 782-1967
Chatsworth, CA
www.lampsplus.com
Indoor and outdoor lighting

MP Global Products
(888) 379-9695
Norfolk, NE
www.mpglobalproducts.com
KwikDek patio duckboards

QC Construction Products
(800) 453-8213
Madera, CA
www.qcconprod.com
Concrete colorants, cures, sealers

**Quality Systems, Inc./
PermaCrete**
(800) 607-3762
Nashville, TN
www.permacrete.com
Concrete resurfacing

ShadeTree Systems, LLC
(800) 894-3801
Columbus, OH
www.shadetreecanopies.com
Retractable awnings

Smith & Hawken
(800) 940-1170
Novato, CA
www.smithandhawken.com
Outdoor furniture and accessories

Sonoma Cast Stone
(888) 807-4234
Sonoma, CA
www.sonomastone.com
Architectural concrete products

SunPorch Structures, Inc.
(203) 454-0040
Westport, CT
www.sunporch.com
Sunroom and screened room kits

SunSetter Awnings
(800) 491-0911
Malden, MA
www.sunsetter.com
Retractable awnings

**Sure-loc Edging/
Wolverine Products**
(800) 787-3562
Holland, MI
www.surelocedging.com
Aluminum landscape edging

credits

PHOTOGRAPHY CREDITS

Em Ahart: 64 middle left; Paul Bardagjy: 48; Beateworks/Tim Street-Porter: 160 top; Marion Brenner: 67 top left, 80 bottom right, 121 all; Brian Vanden Brink: 106 middle right; Wayne Cable: 117 top right (3), 168–170 all, 171 top right and middle right, 172 bottom, 173–174 all; courtesy of Cal Spas: 82 top; Rob Cardillo: 29 bottom, 143 top; James Carrier: 52 both; David Cavagnaro: 23 middle, 67 middle left, 81 top right, 158 top, 163 bottom right; Todd Caverly: 105 bottom right; Crandall & Crandall: 103 center; Rosalind Creasy: 96, 97 top; R. Todd Davis: 111 top; Janet Davis: 165 bottom; Alan & Linda Detrick: 11 left, 92, 93 top, 120; courtesy of Dig Corporation: 63 top right and middle right; Liz Eddison/The Garden Collection: 33 bottom right; Cheryl Fenton: 45, 74 bottom (3), 75 top (3), 102 top right (3), 155 all; Scott Fitzgerrell: 116 (4); Roger Foley: 7 bottom right; 10 left, 15 top, 15 bottom left, 16, 17 bottom right, 19 left, 23 top, 25 left and bottom right, 28 bottom, 31 top, 32 top, 54, 56, 101 top, 108 top, 166; Frank Gaglione: 76 all, 77 top, 84, 87 top, 98 bottom, 99 top right, 100 top, 103 bottom, 104 bottom, 105 top right, 107 inset, 116 (6), 117 (10), 122–123 all, 125 both, 127 all, 131 both, 135 top, 136 all, 138–139 all, 140 middle right and bottom right, 141 all, 142 center and bottom, 143 bottom left and bottom right, 144–154 all, 156 bottom center and bottom right, 157 all, 159 center and bottom, 161 all, 162 bottom, 164 bottom left and bottom right, 165 top left, top center and top right, 167, 175 all, 177 all, 178 bottom, 179 all, 187 both, 188 all; courtesy of Gloster Furniture: 2 bottom, 34 bottom, 50 bottom left, 51 bottom, 189; courtesy of Grupo Kettal/Evolutif: 51 top; Positive Images/Gay Bumgarner: 12 top; Positive Images/Karen Bussolini: 19 top right; Steven Gunther: 60 top right, 158 bottom right, 171 bottom left, 172 top; Philip Harvey: 43, 107 bottom, 119 glasses; Saxon Holt: 1, 2 top, 3 top left, 4, 6 right, 8 bottom, 17 top, 18 top, 21 bottom left, 30 top and middle, 33 top right, 38, 67 bottom left, 78 both, 80 top right, 88 top left, 90, 91 top, 94, 95 bottom, 106 top left, 107 top, 163 bottom left; courtesy of Infrared Dynamics: 36 bottom right; Douglas Johnson: 15 bottom right, 24 top, 99 middle right, 104 top, 168; Robert Kourik/TerraInforma Communications: 63 bottom right; Dennis Krukowski: 47; courtesy of KwikDek by MP Global Products: 126 all; courtesy of

LAMPS PLUS/LAMPSPLUS.com: 72 bottom (4); Janet Loughrey: 3 bottom, 7 top left, 10 right, 13 bottom, 20, 31 bottom, 35 bottom, 178 top; Allan Mandell: 3 top right, 6 left, 7 top right, 8 top, 9, 12 bottom, 13 top right, 22, 66, 67 top right, 80 left, 102 bottom left, 160 bottom, 176; Charles Mann: 23 bottom; Mise au Point/N. and P. Mioulane: 124, 132 top, 156 top, 158 bottom left; Mise au Point/Yann Monel: 21 bottom left; Mise au Point/C. Nichols: 11 top right, 14, 21 top left, 73 left and bottom center, 142 top, 159 top, 164; Mise au Point/Noun: 32 bottom, 67 bottom right; Mise au Point/F. Strauss: 21 top right; Jerry Pavia: 134; Norm Plate: 3 middle, 19 bottom right, 24 bottom, 28 top, 30 bottom, 68–71 all, 88 bottom, 89 top, 100 bottom; courtesy of QC Construction: 81 bottom; courtesy of Rapid Cool: 37; Phillip C. Roullard: 64 top left; Mark Rutherford: 73 right, 119 gloves; Loren Santow: 61, 62 all, 63 top left, 64 center, bottom center and right, 65 all, 75 bottom, 79 all, 99 top center and bottom right (3), 102 middle right, 106 bottom, 118, 132 bottom, 133 all, 182–186 all; Michael Skott: 60 bottom and top left, 98 top, 140 top; courtesy of ShadeTree Systems: 26, 27 top left; courtesy of Smith & Hawken: 34 top, 35 top left and top right, 36 middle right, 50 top, 51 middle; courtesy of Sonoma Cast Stone: 103 top right; Thomas J. Story: 25 top right, 36 top left, 58, 59 all, 83, 116 digging bar, 128, 129 all; Dan Stultz: 87 middle and bottom, 112 top; courtesy of www.SunPorch.com: 46 both, 47 top and middle; courtesy of SunSetter Awnings: 27 top right and middle right; Michael S. Thompson: 18 bottom, 72 top left, 73 top center, 99 bottom left, 103 top left; Dave Toht: 86 all; E. Spencer Toy: 50 middle right; Mark Turner: 13 top left; Christopher Vendetta: 55 all, 57 all; Jessie Walker: 27 bottom right, 29 top, 33 middle left, 82 bottom, 130; Karen Witynski: 11 bottom right, 17 bottom left, 105 bottom left, 111 bottom

DESIGN CREDITS

Monty Anderson, Architect, and Rosalind Creasy, Landscape Designer: 96, 97 top; Suzanne Arca: 90, 91 top; Arentz Landscape Architects: 7 bottom right, 19 left, 23 top, 31 top, 166; A. Wear Associates: 14; Jeff Bale: 176; Troy Bankord: 23 bottom; Shari Bashin-Sullivan/ Enchanting Planting: 4, 30 middle and bottom; Rick Bayless: 23 middle; Jill Billington: 142 top; Linda Brown: 29 top; Scott Brunton: 3 bottom; Bunny Williams, Inc.: 47; Tom Chakas and Roger Raiche: 8 top; Jack Chandler: 78 top; Bob Chittock: 67 top right; Ruth Chivers: 21 top

left; Jeff Clark: 178 top; Clinton & Associates: 25 left, 28 bottom; Cording Landscape Design: 92, 93 top; Laura Crockett: 10 right; Nancy Driscoll: 1, 8 bottom; Jay Ferguson: 3 middle, 19 bottom right; Sonny Garcia: 33 top right; Jeff Glander: 12 bottom; Franz Goebel: 88 bottom right; Will Goodman and Michael Schultz: 102 bottom left; Steve Gossett: 100 bottom; Richard Haag: 38; Donna Hackman: 15 top, 16, 32 top; Stefan Hammerschmidt: 60 top right; Lucy Hardiman: 7 top left, 13 bottom; Thomas Hobbs and Brent Beattie: 7 top right; Cathy Hoekman/Concept Landscapes: 22; Huettl Thuilot Associates: 28 top; Chris Jacobson: 94, 95 bottom, 107 top; Johnsen Landscapes & Pools: 19 top right; Lankford Associates: 43; Lindsay Lee/Willowglen Nursery: 163 bottom right; Michael Levine: 120; Colin Lichtensteiger and Steve Ansell: 80 left; David Little and George Lewis: 160 bottom; Logan Pools: 99 middle right; Nicole Lopez: 171 bottom left; Julie Moir Messervy: 6 left, 66; Mary Morgan: 111 top; Nancy Hammer Landscape Design: 106 top left; Harry North and Jeff Sargent/Creative Environments: 88 top left; Oehme, Van Sweden & Associates: 10 left, 101 top; Pamela Dreyfuss Interior Design and Exteriors Landscape Architecture: 25 top right, 83; Rick Peters: 54, 56; Piedmont Designs: 29 bottom; Poly-Scapes Landscape Construction & Design: 36 top left; Alvaro Ponce: 105 bottom left; Suzanne Porter: 21 bottom left; Putnam Construction & Landscaping: 158 bottom right; Hamida Betty Rahman: 20; Raymond Jungles Landscape Architect: 108 top; Mary Reid: 6 right; Dean Riddle: 11 left; Jim Ripley: 70; Sarah Robertson: 99 bottom left; Linda Searl: 27 bottom right; Doug Shock/The Patio Pros: 103 top left; Scott Simons, Architect: 106 middle right; George Snead Jr., Designer: 105 bottom right; Brad Stangland: 72 top left, 73 top center; Bud Stuckey: 128; Tekton Architecture: 15 bottom right; Michael Thilgen: 17 top, 67 bottom left, 163 bottom left; Scott Thurmon: 111 bottom; Tom Mannion Landscape Design: 15 bottom left, 25 bottom right; Charles Travis/Travis Architects: 48; Suzanne Van Atta: 18 top; Viscusi-Elson Design and Noel Cross, Architect: 24 top; Ron Wagner and Nani Waddoups: 3 top right, 9; Bruce Wakefield and Jerry Grossnickle: 13 top right; Peter O. Whiteley: 52; William Wood Architects: 168; Stephen Woodhams: 11 top right; David Yakish: 3 top left, 78 bottom, 80 top right; Yunghi Choi Landscape Architect: 17 bottom right; Jeff Zischke/Zischke Studio: 24 bottom

index